INVENTORY AND MONITORING
Technical Reference 1734-7

Ecological Site Inventory

December 2001

By:

Edward F. Habich
Rangeland Management Specialist
Bureau of Land Management
National Science and Technology Center
Denver, Colorado

U.S. Department of the Interior · Bureau of Land Management

"An ecological site is a distinctive kind of land with specific physical characteristics that differs from others kinds of land in its ability to produce a distinctive kind and amount of vegetation."

–National Range and Pasture Handbook

Suggested citation:

Habich, E.F. 2001. Ecological site inventory, Technical reference 1734-7. Bureau of Land Management. Denver, Colorado. BLM/ST/ST-01/003+1734. 112 pp.

UNITED STATES DEPARTMENT OF THE INTERIOR
BUREAU OF LAND MANAGEMENT
NATIONAL SCIENCE AND TECHNOLOGY CENTER
DENVER FEDERAL CENTER, BUILDING 50
P.O. BOX 25047
DENVER, COLORADO 80225-0047
September 27, 2002

In Reply Refer To:
1734(ST-132) **P**

EMS Transmission
Information Bulletin No. ST-2002-106

To: All Field Officials

From: Director, National Science and Technology Center

Subject: Methods for Determining Plot-Based Aboveground Vegetation Production

Three methods for estimating aboveground vegetation production are presented on pages 37 to 41 in Technical Reference 1734-7 (hereinafter referred to as TR approach), Ecological Site Inventory, published in 2001. Two of these three methods are also presented on pages 102 to 115 in Technical Reference 1734-4, Sampling Vegetation Attributes, published most recently in 1999. These methods are each plot-based. For each of these methods, direction is given to include current-year portions of plants lying within the vertical projections of the plot boundary in the production estimate, and conversely, all portions of plants lying outside the plot boundary are excluded (see Figure 4 on page 37 in Technical Reference 1734-7).

The Natural Resources Conservation Service (NRCS), on pages 4-4 to 4-7 in the 1997 National Range and Pasture Handbook, presents a different approach. The NRCS directs that plants with bases which originate within the plot boundary are identified, and current-year portions of these plants are included in the production estimate, even if some of these portions lie outside the plot boundary. Conversely, plants with bases which originate outside the plot boundary might have portions which lie within the vertical projections of the plot boundary, but these portions are not included. This approach is also presented in BLM's National Range Handbook, H-4410-1 (hereinafter referred to as Handbook approach), published most recently in 1984 (see Exhibit 604.3(e)(1) in H-4410-1).

There is inconsistency between the TR approach and the Handbook approach. The change made by the BLM in Technical References 1734-4 and 1734-7 was to provide an alternative approach for estimating aboveground vegetation production for field use across ecological sites dominated by grasses, forbs, or shrubs. A perusal of literature and professional judgment of rangeland scientists on the subject of sampling of vegetation production provide evidence that neither approach of estimating vegetation production is incorrect. National Academy of Sciences—National Research Council (1962), Mueller-Dombois and Ellenberg (1974), Pieper (1978), Cook and Stubbendieck (1986), and Elzinga et al. (1998), all contain discussions about sampling methods for estimating vegetation production, but none disclose detailed information on which portions of plants should be associated with the plot area. Ruyle (1997), however, recommends the same approach as that found in the TR approach.

The strengths and weaknesses of each approach are somewhat related to the life form of vegetation which is being estimated across an existing vegetation type. For vegetation types dominated by grasses and grass-like plants, the Handbook approach would appear to be the stronger approach. Grass tissue can droop with moisture stress and can become more erect when hydrated. Movement of grass tissue in this manner can affect the amount of tissue lying within the vertical projections of the plot boundary, if the TR approach is used. This problem would not surface using the Handbook approach because the entire portion of the plant is estimated, even if a portion of the plant lies outside the plot boundary, as long as the plant is rooted within the plot area.

For vegetation types where shrubs are prevalent, the TR approach would appear to be the stronger approach. There can be instances where shrub individuals can be rooted within a plot boundary, yet very little of the aboveground production can actually lie within the vertical projections of the plot boundary. Using the Handbook approach in this instance, the amount of aboveground production associated with the plot area would be overestimated.

For vegetation types where tall shrubs and trees, for example, pinon and juniper are prevalent, aboveground vegetation production methods are generally not suitable (Ruyle 1997). Using the TR approach, the vertical projections of the plot boundary must be visually projected upward, which is comparatively more difficult than visually projecting the plot boundary downward. The Handbook approach still suffers here as well because tall shrubs and trees can be rooted within the plot boundary, yet most of their aboveground production can lie outside the plot area.

In summary, neither of the two approaches is solely the preferred choice. Each approach, if used to estimate vegetation production for an existing vegetation type, is likely similar in accuracy. **An important consideration with either approach is consistency in use over time and data standardization.** With renewed interest in FY 2002 from Congress on devising standardized monitoring and assessment methodologies, there might be a need to further refine these approaches to achieve a greater degree of consistency between agencies. Until such time, recommendations are to: (1) continue using the Handbook approach if the Handbook approach has been the traditional choice, and if data sharing or sharing data collection responsibility with the NRCS has been commonplace or (2) continue using the TR approach if the TR approach has been the traditional choice.

If you have any questions regarding this information bulletin, please contact Mike "Sherm" Karl at (303) 236-0166.

Signed by: Authenticated by:
Lee Barkow, Director   Elsie Pacheco
National Science and   Staff Assistant
Technology Center

1 Attachment
    1 – References (1 p)

Distribution
ST-150, BLM Library

References

Cook, C.W., and J. Stubbendieck. 1986. Range research: basic problems and techniques. Society for Range Management, Denver, CO. 317 pp. + introduction.

Elzinga, C.L., D.W. Salzer, and J.W. Willoughby. 1998. Measuring and monitoring plant populations. Technical Reference 1730-1, U.S. Department of the Interior, Bureau of Land Management, National Science and Technology Center, Lakewood, CO. 477 pp. + introduction.

Mueller-Dombois, D., and H. Ellenberg. 1974. Aims and methods of vegetation ecology. John Wiley & Sons, New York. 547 pp.

National Academy of Sciences—National Research Council. 1962. Basic problems and techniques in range research. Publication No. 890. Washington, D.C. 341 pp. + introduction.

Pieper, R.D. 1978. Measurement techniques for herbaceous and shrubby vegetation. New Mexico State University, Las Cruces. 148 pp.

Ruyle, G.B. (editor). 1997. Some methods for monitoring rangelands and other natural area vegetation. Arizona Cooperative Extension Publication 190043, Cooperative Extension, College of Agriculture, The University of Arizona, Tucson.

Preface

SINCE DECEMBER 1982, ecological site inventory (ESI) has been the Bureau of Land Management's (BLM) standard vegetation inventory technique. The ecological site inventory method involves the use of soils information to map ecological sites and plant communities and the collection of natural resource and vegetation attributes. The sampling data from each of these soil-vegetation units, referred to as site write-up areas (SWAs), become the baseline data for natural resource management and planning.

The purpose of Technical Reference 1734-7, *Ecological Site Inventory*, is to identify the procedures for completing an ecological site inventory and to describe the technique used by the Natural Resource Conservation Service (NRCS) to document and describe ecological sites. These procedures were derived from the NRCS Rangeland Ecological Site Inventory procedure as described in their *National Range and Pasture Handbook*. Information was also adapted from the NRCS National Soils Handbook and BLM Technical Reference 1737-7, *Procedures for Ecological Site Inventory—With Special Reference to Riparian-Wetland Sites*. Technical Reference 1734-7 replaces previous guidance found in BLM Manual Handbook 4410-1.

The need for natural resource inventories are mandated by Congress in Section 201(a) of the Federal Land Policy and Management Act (FLPMA) of 1976. Congress reaffirmed this need in Section 4 of the Public Rangelands Improvement Act (PRIA) of 1978—in particular, to develop and maintain an inventory of range conditions and trends on public rangelands, and to keep that inventory updated on a regular basis.

Table of Contents

Preface i

Chapter 1 - Inventory 1
  Inventory Preparation 1
    Inventory Plan 1
      Table 1 - Inventory Plan Format 2
    Inventory Plan Reviews 4
    Inventory Team 4
      Figure 1 - Composition of Inventory Team 4
      Team Lead 5
      Soil Survey Team 5
      Vegetation Mapping Team 5
      Vegetation Transecting Team 5
      Phenological Data Collection Team 5
      Natural Resource Specialists on the Inventory Team ... 5
  Preparing for Field Operations 7
    Training and Orientation 7
    Aerial Photographs and Maps 8
      Aerial Photographs 8
      Orthophoto Quads 8
      Topographic and Planimetric Maps 8
      Administrative Maps 9
      Other Maps 9
      Remote Sensing Imagery 9
    General Equipment 9
      Table 2 - Equipment List 10
    Specialized Equipment 11
      Soils 11
      Vegetation 11
      Wildlife Biology 12
      Hydrology 12

Chapter 2 - Soils 15
  Soil Map Unit 15
    Consociation 15
    Complex 15
    Association 15
    Undifferentiated Group 16
  Soil Map Unit Development 16

Soil Map Unit Descriptions 16
Detailed Soil Maps 16
Soil Survey Mapping for Riparian-Wetland Areas 17
   Figure 2 - Schematic Representation of Soil Map with Line Segments 17
Importance of Soil Map Units 18

Chapter 3 - Ecological Sites 19
Definition of Ecological Site 19
Succession and Retrogression 19
States and Transition Pathways 20
   Figure 3 - State and Transition Model Diagram for an Ecological Site 20
Historic Climax Plant Community 22
Naturalized Plant Community 22
Potential Natural Community 23
Historic Climax Plant Community Versus Potential Natural Community 23
Changes in Ecological Site Potential 23
Characteristic Vegetation States of an Ecological Site 24
Differentiation Between Ecological Sites 24
Revising Ecological Site Descriptions 26
Developing New Ecological Site Descriptions 26
BLM Procedures 26
Naming Ecological Sites on Rangeland 26
Numbering Ecological Sites 27
Correlating Ecological Sites 28
Ecological Site Description 28
   Heading 28
   Ecological Site Name 28
   Ecological Site ID 28
   Major Land Resource Area 28
   Interstate Correlation 28
   Physiographic Features 28
   Climatic Features 29
   Influencing Water Features 29
   Representative Soil Features 29
   Ecological Dynamics of the Site 29
   Plant Communities 29
   Species List 30
   Plant Groups 30
   Cover and Structure 31
      Table 3 - Cover and Structure 31
   Biological Soil Crust Communities 32
   Total Annual Production 32

Plant Community Growth Curves 32
    Table 4 - Plant Community Growth Curves 32
Ecological Site Interpretations 32
    Animal Community 32
    Hydrologic Functions 33
    Recreational Uses 33
    Wood Products 33
    Other Products 33
    Supporting Information 33
    Associated Sites 33
    Similar Sites 33
    Inventory Data References 33
    State Correlation 33
    Type Locality 33
    Relationship to Other Established Classification Systems 33
    Other References 33
    Ecological Site Documentation and References 33
        Authorship 34
        Site Approval 34
Forestland Ecological Sites 34
Separating Forested Lands from Rangelands in Areas Where They Interface 34

Chapter 4 - Production Data 35
Aboveground Vegetation Production 35
Total Annual Production 35
Production for Various Kinds of Plants 35
    Herbaceous Plants 36
    Woody Plants 36
    Cacti 36
Methods of Determining Production 37
    Figure 4 - Weight Estimate Plots 37
Estimating by Weight Units 38
Double Sampling—Estimating and Harvesting 39
    Table 5 - Number of Harvested Plots 39
    Plot Size 40
    Plot Shape 40
Harvesting 41
Units of Production and Conversion Factors 41
Plot Size Conversion Factors 41
    Table 6 - Conversion Factors for Grams to Pounds per Acre 41
    Table 7 - Conversion Factors for Grams to Kilograms per Hectare 42
    Mixed Measuring Units 42

Adjustment Factors 42
   Green Weight Adjustment Factor 42
   Double Sampling Adjustment Factor 43
   Air-dry Weight Adjustment Factor 43
   Utilization Adjustment Factor 43
   Growth Adjustment Factor 43
Reconstructing the Present Plant Community .43
Ocular Estimation of Production Data 44
Inventory Level of Intensity 44
Production Data for Documenting Rangeland Ecological Sites 44

Chapter 5 - Similarity Index 45
Definition and Purpose of a Similarity Index 45
   Table 8 - Successional Status 45
Determining Similarity Index 45
   Table 9 - Examples of Similarity Index Determinations on a Loamy Upland 12-16 PZ
     Ecological Site 47
   Table 10 - Reference Community 51
Determining Similarity Index to the Potential Natural Community 52
Determining Similarity Index to Other Vegetation States or Desired Plant Community 52

Chapter 6 - Field Procedures 53
Minimum Standards 53
Sampling Precision 53
Site Write-up Area 53
Field Inventory Mapping 54
Mapping Process With a Completed Soil Survey 54
Mapping Process Without a Completed Soil Survey 55
Mapping Ecological Sites 55
Present Vegetation 55
   Table 11 - Common Standard Vegetation Subtypes 55
Successional Status Classification 56
Forest Types 56
Feature Mapping 56
Water Resources 56
Photo Scale 56
   Table 12 - Photo Scale Minimum Size Delineations 56
Stratification 56
   Table 13 - Recommended Protocols for Stratification 57
   Table 14 - Stratum Listing and SWA Listing by Stratum 57
   Stratums With One Transect 58
   Stratums With Multiple Transects 58

Transect Locations 58
   SWAs With One Soil-Vegetation Unit 58
    Figure 5 - One Soil-Vegetation Unit 58
   SWAs With Mixed or Mottled Patterns 59
    Figure 6 - Mixed or Mottled Soil-Vegetation Units 59
   Other Options for Transect Layout 59
    Figure 7a - A Two-Legged Transect 59
    Figure 7b - A Multi-Legged Transect 59
Plot Sampling 60
Vegetation Production Worksheet 60

Chapter 7 - Data Storage 61

Abbreviations and Acronyms 63

Glossary 65

Bibliography 73

Appendix 1 - Aerial Photography 75

Appendix 2 - Soil Map Unit Delineations 77

Appendix 3 - Ecological Site Description 81

Appendix 4 - Vegetation Production Worksheet 97

Appendix 5 - Foliage Denseness Classes Utah Juniper 99

Appendix 6 - Examples of Weight Units 101

Appendix 7 - Percent Air-dry Weight Conversion Table 103

Appendix 8 - Vegetation Types and Subtypes 105

Appendix 9 - Similarity Index Form 107

Appendix 10 - Data Element Codes 109

Chapter 1 - Inventory

Inventory Preparation

ADEQUATE INVENTORY PREPARATION is essential for all ecological site inventories. Inventory preparation should be initiated at least 1 year prior to the start of field work; however, 2 years is better and is usually required if memorandums of understanding (MOUs) or other agreements are necessary for interagency efforts. Inventory preparation includes developing an inventory plan, conducting inventory plan reviews, and putting together the inventory team.

Inventory Plan

Prior to beginning an inventory, an interdisciplinary team develops the inventory plan. The team sets forth in writing the extent and intensity of the inventory studies needed. The ecological site inventory is designed to serve as the basic inventory of present and potential vegetation on BLM rangelands for use in all programs that require information on vegetation.

The level of intensity for the collection of production data should be documented in the inventory plan, along with a discussion about quality control of data collection. This is necessary to ensure accuracy and promote consistency between crews and inventories.

If a Natural Resources Conservation Service (NRCS) soil survey or soil survey update is conducted along with an inventory, the plan should be consistent with the soil survey MOU and plan of operations according to Section 601.05 of the *National Soils Handbook*. (See the section on soil survey for information on the procedure needed if a soil survey is completed concurrently with the ecological site inventory.)

A suggested format for the inventory plan is shown in Table 1.

Table 1 - Inventory Plan Format

Inventory Plan Elements

Purpose	Briefly state the purpose of the inventory in general terms.
Objective(s)	Identify the specific objective(s) for the inventory data in relation to uses or issues.
Description of the inventory area	Identify the location and boundaries. Describe what it looks like (vegetation diversity, topographic diversity).
Identify information to be collected	Although the minimum standards required for an ESI are production and composition by air-dry weight (ADW) by species, all other types of resource data can be collected. Data collection should be tailored to local needs. Inventory protocols can be specifically designed for certain areas within the inventory. Additional data needs could include: - Cover - Vegetation structure - Rangeland health - Soil resource values and condition (soil health) - Tree information (number by size, class, types of tree damage and extent) - Noxious weeds - Biological soil crust
Inventory design	- Identify the level of detail needed. A higher level of detail may be required in riparian-wetland or other high value areas. - Specify map scale. Different scales may be required in mapping uplands and riparian-wetland areas. - Specify the minimum size limitation for delineating soil map units and site write-up areas (SWAs). For example, a soil map unit may be no smaller than 160 acres (for a general order 3 survey), while a SWA may be as small as 40 acres. - Determine whether the inventory will be completed in conjunction with a soil survey or after the soil survey is complete. - Determine the time that will be needed to complete the field work and all compilation work.
Personnel and funding requirements and/or constraints	- People and skill levels needed (professional level versus seasonal or entry level) - Personnel assigned to complete the work - Special needs (helicopter support, equipment)

Logistics	- Aerial photo or remote sensing needs - Agreements or MOUs - Transportation (vehicles, helicopter) - Office space - Chemical storage space (HCL, pH reagents) - Lodging (camps, motels) - Food or per diem requirements - Equipment, photos, maps (some procurement may be needed 1 year in advance) - Contracts - Administrative support - Coordination with local officials and notification in the local newspaper, particularly if helicopters are used
Field measurements and procedures	- Minimum standards. Production and composition by species, by SWA, and by ecological site are required. - Number and size of plots - Other data collection methods to be used (Daubenmire, step point, line intercept, point frame) - Handbooks and other written guidance - Data collection (forms, field data recorders)
Compilation procedures	- Maps - Cartographic requirements - Geographic Information System (GIS) support - Data storage. Method of tabular data input into the Inventory Data System (IDS) (local entry into Bureau database) - Types of reports to be generated and for whom
Reporting and quality control (inventory reviews and results) requirements	- Training - Sampling and harvesting protocols - Personnel supervision in the field - Frequency of progress reports (weekly, monthly) - Who is responsible and when progress and final reports are due
Approval Process	- Who the responsible individuals are - When - What the administrative levels are
File Maintenance	Identify where the field worksheets, maps, and reports will be stored and plans for computerizing the data. Data must be entered in the Bureau's vegetation database. To determine how it will be entered, contact the National Science and Technology Center (NSTC) in Denver.

Inventory Plan Reviews

The inventory plan needs to be reviewed annually if the inventory takes longer than 1 year to complete. All changes should be documented. The inventory plan should set forth when and how reviews will be conducted. The inventory team should conduct the reviews. Objectives should be reviewed to ensure adequate quality and quantity of inventory progress and to identify problems that need management attention.

Inventory Team

The inventory team generally consists of a team lead, a soil survey team, a vegetation mapping team, a vegetation transecting team, and a phenological data collection team. A soil survey team may not be necessary if the survey is already done. Also, if specified in the inventory plan, the soil survey and vegetation mapping teams may be combined into a single team to complete the mapping of the inventory area. Figure 1, Composition of Inventory Team, is only a recommendation. Composition of the actual teams will be decided by each individual field office.

Inventory team members must be selected carefully. The combined knowledge, experience, education, and training of each member is extremely important. All specialists on the inventory team will need to work closely together throughout the inventory.

Ecological Site Inventory Team Organization

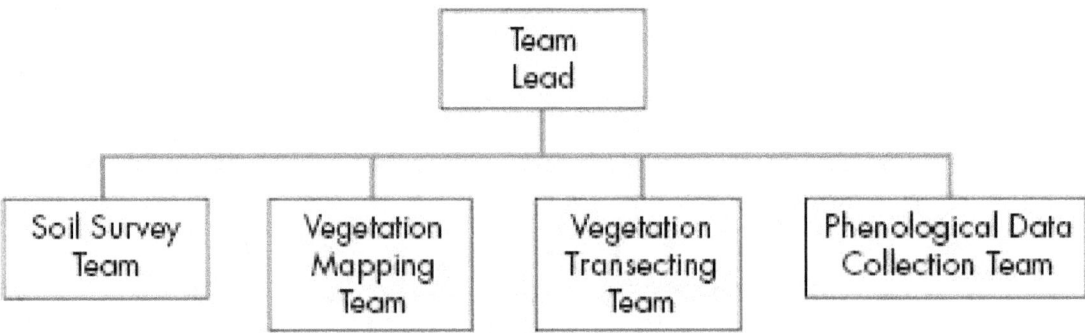

Figure 1 - Composition of Inventory Team

Team Lead

The team lead should be a BLM permanent employee with supervisory experience. Leads should be selected for their knowledge, experience, competence, and good judgment. They should be knowledgeable and experienced in the objectives and procedures of ecological site inventories and acquainted with the Bureau's interrelated programs. They are responsible for organizing and directing the inventory, coordinating field data collection, assigning work, keeping equipment in good operating order, administrative support (time sheets, leave approval, employee evaluations, travel, training) and reporting the progress of the inventory.

Soil Survey Team

The soil survey team is needed only if a soil survey has not been completed or if the existing survey needs further refinement. The team may include employees from BLM, NRCS, combined BLM-NRCS, or contract personnel.

Vegetation Mapping Team

The vegetation mapping team usually works in close contact with the soil survey team and is responsible for the delineation of ecological sites, successional status, and present vegetation communities. Team members should include an experienced vegetation management specialist (e.g., rangeland management specialist, forester, ecologist, botanist), a soil scientist, and a wildlife biologist. If riparian-wetland sites are involved in the inventory, a hydrologist is critical, at least during the planning, soil survey, and vegetation mapping phases. These specialists must be familiar with the soils and plant and animal communities of the inventory area.

Vegetation Transecting Team

The vegetation transecting team is usually comprised of rangeland management specialists, biologists, botanists, and foresters. A knowledge of the plants in the inventory area is required, along with a good plant taxonomy background. Botany expertise may be required full or part time. For riparian-wetland inventory updates, at least one vegetation specialist with experience in wetland ecology and wetland plant taxonomy is needed.

Phenological Data Collection Team

It may be desirable to assign the responsibility of collecting data for phenological adjustment factors to one or two individuals. This will ensure accurate data collection in a timely manner for this important phase of the inventory. This team may also collect samples for air-dry weight (ADW) conversion data.

Natural Resource Specialists on the Inventory Team

The following natural resource specialists can provide the necessary experience and expertise as part of the individual teams that form the main inventory team.

Soil Scientist

The soil scientist is responsible for mapping ecological sites and developing soil map units.

Vegetation Management Specialist

The vegetation management specialist is responsible for mapping vegetation communities and administrative boundaries; collecting vegetation and related resource data (e.g., production, cover, rangeland health, structure); and assisting the soil scientist in mapping ecological sites and developing soil map units.

The vegetation management specialist can be a botanist, biologist, rangeland management specialist, forester, or anyone proficient in identifying vegetation species. This expertise is usually involved to some degree on all phases of the inventory (i.e., vegetation mapping, soil survey, transecting, and phenology) including inventory plan preparation.

Wildlife Biologist

The wildlife biologist is responsible for ensuring that wildlife issues and concerns are considered in the mapping of ecological sites and vegetation communities. This includes noting special habitat features on aerial photos. Features to be mapped will have been determined in the pre- planning analysis and inventory plan, which will identify the areas to be investigated in detail after the inventory is complete.

Input from a wildlife biologist is recommended throughout ecological site inventories and soil surveys. Although not involved during all the field mapping, the wildlife biologist needs to have direct input at critical times, which include the initial planning phase and area base map preparation; map unit design to ensure that wildlife habitat vegetation components are recognized and wildlife interpretation needs are met; ecological site description interpretation development and revision; and development of applicable soil-wildlife-habitat interpretations. Because of the extremely high wildlife values associated with riparian-wetland areas, the wildlife biologist's participation in field mapping is critical and participation in riparian-wetland ecological site inventories and updates is required. In addition, the wildlife biologist provides assistance to other members of the inventory team (e.g., hydrologist) in completing the field work for developing ecological site descriptions, and is also involved in inventory plan preparations.

Hydrologist

A hydrologist is an integral part of the inventory team relative to riparian-wetland sites. The hydrologist is responsible for the description of water features associated with riparian-wetland map units and ecological sites. Hydrologic input for progressive soil surveys and ecological site inventories is critical during the planning phase and in map unit design to ensure accurate watershed hydrologic interpretations. The hydrologist's input in mapping, describing, and updating riparian-wetland ecological sites is required.

The hydrologist works with the soil scientist and vegetation management specialist to establish interrelationships and ecological responses to hydrologic events and changes over time and space attributable to stream dynamics or other surface and near-surface water fluctuations.

Other Resource Specialists

Input from other natural resource specialists and managers, other than those mentioned previously, should be actively sought to identify specific needs whenever necessary. Their input is especially valuable during the inventory planning phase and again in the development of site and soil interpretations. In addition, assistance from recreation specialists, geologists, geomorphologists, fire managers, and other natural resource specialists are often helpful throughout the inventory and site description processes depending on the complexity and resource values associated with individual areas.

Preparing for Field Operations

The team lead formulates a plan of operation, assembles materials and equipment, makes necessary arrangements, and coordinates with appropriate field office staff. The lead is responsible for ensuring that all forms, maps, photos, and other equipment and supplies necessary for conducting the inventory are available.

Training and Orientation

The training and orientation of the inventory team is the responsibility of the team lead. The lead is responsible for assessing specific training needs. This includes scheduling and preparing training in procedures (e.g., mapping units, data collection, plant identification, aerial photo interpretation). It also includes orientation to the geographical inventory area and rangeland users.

It is particularly important that the inventory team be well trained on measurement techniques. The inventory team should have a basic understanding of the kinds and amount of data needed and the intended uses of the data.

The need for training in specific sampling techniques for each discipline represented in an ecological site inventory will vary greatly depending on individual background and expertise.

The following are recommended courses:

• Inventory and Monitoring of Plant Populations (BLM National Training Center (NTC) Course 1730-05). Presents information on inventory, monitoring, analysis, and evaluation techniques for vegetation and plant populations.

• The Ecological Site Concept (BLM NTC Course 4000-ST-2, self-study course and video). Provides basic instruction on soil map units, ecological site concepts, and SWA mapping criteria.

• Coordinated Riparian Area Management (BLM NTC Course 1737-1). Provides an introduction to riparian-wetland ecological site concepts, as well as substantial information on BLM riparian-wetland policies, values, and management concepts.

• Riparian-Wetland Ecological Site Classification (BLM NTC Course 1737-4). Advanced course for mapping and describing riparian-wetland sites.

• GIS - Geodata for Resource Specialists (BLM NTC Course 1730-11). Provides a basic understanding and hands-on experience in the concepts, use, and application of GIS.

• Basic Aerial Phot Interpretation (BLM NTC Course 9160-1). Provides students with the background and ability to interpret and use various kinds of aerial photography.

• Soils - Basic Soil Survey: Field and Laboratory (NRCS National Employee Development Center (NEDC), Fort Worth). Designed to provide new soil scientists and other specialists an opportunity to experience what it takes to complete a soil survey. Output potential of soil interpretations and use of field and laboratory methods and data analysis in soil survey are also discussed.

Additional courses recommended for specific disciplines include:

- ECS - Range Plant Ecology (NRCS NEDC, Fort Worth). Advanced course that provides information on the ecological interaction of range vegetation.

- RES CONS - Saline and Sodic Soils (NRCS NEDC, Fort Worth). Provides a background and hands-on experience in understanding chemical relationships, testing and analyzing data, recognizing problems, and recommending management solutions.

- Soils - Soil Correlation (NRCS NEDC, Fort Worth). Advanced course for soil scientists provides insight and techniques to apply soil classification, soil correlation procedure, geomorphic relationships, soil survey area handbook development, and laboratory data analysis and sampling procedures.

- Soils - Soil Lab Data Use (NRCS NEDC, Fort Worth). Advanced course for soil scientists provides insight and techniques for using laboratory data in soil classification and plant relationships.

- Soils - National Soil Information System (NASIS) (NRCS). Advanced course for soil scientists familiarizes students with NASIS structure, spreadsheet organization, and how to populate NASIS data fields.

Aerial Photographs and Maps

Aerial photographs and maps are important tools in the inventory process. They help identify locations of natural landscape and special features and assist in mapping soils, vegetation communities, and special habitat features.

Aerial Photographs

It is essential to have a complete set of aerial photographs for inventory purposes. These should be acquired well in advance of the inventory. To facilitate the inventory, more recent (less than 10 years old) photos are the most desirable. Natural color or color-infrared photography is best for mapping vegetation, and a scale of 1:24,000 is best suited for ease of transferring the information to orthophoto quads or topographic maps. The aerial photos or orthophoto quads are used for field mapping and this information is then transferred to the map base. Aerial photos are helpful in seeing greater detail, but orthophotos are better for mapping. Refer to Appendix 1 for details on acquiring aerial photos.

Orthophoto Quads

Orthophoto quads are distortion-free image maps at 1:24,000 scale. They are excellent tools for mapping data in the field or from aerial photography. They can also be scanned and georeferenced for inclusion in GIS. With an ortho image as a backdrop, the user can digitize the inventory units, display global positioning system (GPS) data, or analyze other data layers. Also available in most areas are Digital Ortho Quarter Quads (DOQQ), which have replaced paper and film orthophotos and are GIS-ready images. Contact your State Office GIS coordinator about availability.

Topographic and Planimetric Maps

Use topographic and planimetric maps or any high-quality maps that accurately show the relative position and nature of the inventory area features. U.S. Geological Survey (USGS) topographic quadrangles at 1:24,000 scale are the most useable and available. They, too, come in digital format for GIS and are called USGS Digital Raster Graphics (DRG).

Administrative Maps

Administrative maps include information such as management units or grazing allotment boundaries, range improvements, timber harvests, fish and wildlife habitat, and land status. They are useful references for team members during the inventory and can be integrated as data layers for analysis in GIS if they have been digitized. Overlays can be made for use with orthophoto quads as well.

Other Maps

Topographic maps overlaid with geology, precipitation, and land ownership are helpful in mapping soils and ecological sites.

Remote Sensing Imagery

Remote sensing images may be helpful in mapping landscape features, vegetation communities, and soils. Remote sensing images can be obtained at comparable scales to orthophoto quads providing multispectral information.

General Equipment

Equipment and tools include items such as photos, maps, references, forms, pens, pencils, Quadrat frames, and balance scales. Table 2 lists general equipment common to each discipline.

Table 2 - Equipment List

General Equipment	Soils	Vegetation	Wildlife Biology	Hydrology
Inventory plan	x	x	x	x
Memorandum of Understanding (MOU)	x	x	x	x
Manuals and handbooks (see specific lists under Soil, etc.)	x	x	x	x
Forms	x	x	x	x
Field notebook	x	x	x	x
Existing site descriptions common to the inventory area	x	x	x	x
Plant ID references	x	x	x	
List of plant names and symbols found in the State	x	x	x	
Geomorphology reports for the area and related scientific papers	x			
Plat or land status maps	x	x	x	x
Abney level or clinometer	x	x		x
Stereoscope (mirror and pocket)	x	x		
Camera	x	x	x	x
Pens and pencils	x	x	x	x
Compass (magnetic)	x	x		
Quadrat frames		x		
Pin flags		x		
Paper bags		x		
Balance scales		x		
Clippers and grass sheers		x		
Rubber bands		x		
Auger or probe (hand and/or power)	x	x		x
Shovel (standard) and tile spade	x	x		x
Tape measure (metric and English)	x	x	x	x
Computer	x	x	x	x
Vehicle and aircraft	x	x	x	x
First aid kit	x	x	x	x

Specialized Equipment

The following information lists additional equipment and references specific to each discipline.

Soils

Specific soils needs include, but are not limited to:

- Manuals and handbooks on procedural guidance and other references
  - NRCS National Soil Survey Handbook (430-VI-NSSH, 1996)
  - Soil Survey Manual (Agriculture Handbook No. 18, Oct 1993)
  - Soil Taxonomy (2nd edition Agriculture Handbook No. 436 and recent amendments)
  - SMSS Keys to Soil Taxonomy (8th Edition, 1998)
  - NRCS National Range and Pasture Handbook (NRPH)
  - NRCS National Forestry Manual (NFM)
  - NRCS National Biology Manual (NBM)
  - NRCS National Cartographic Manual (NCM)
  - NRCS Field Handbook for Describing and Sampling Soils
  - USDA-NRCS Soil Series of the United States (www.statlab.iastate.edu/soils)
  - State Hydric Soil List
  - For other suggested technical references, see Section 602-4 of the National Soils Handbook (NSH).

- Forms
  - NRCS Field Indicators of Hydric Soils in the United States (Version 4.0, March 1998)
  - Map Unit Transect forms commonly used in the State NRCS-SOI-232 Pedon Description or as revised by the State
  - NRCS-SOI-232F Soil Description or other like forms commonly used in field note taking

- Access to the soil survey database software for data entry into NASIS forms and retrieval

- Field Soil Survey Database (FSSD) for transect management, pedon management, map unit records (NASIS), soils database software

- Pedon description program software

- Equipment
  Altimeter
  Backhoe (mounted on 1-ton truck)
  Color charts (Munsell)
  Digging bar
  Electric conductivity meter
  Geology pick
  Global positions system unit
  Hand lens
  Hydrochloric acid (10% solution)
  Knife
  Light table
  Map board
  pH kit (chemical)
  pH meter
  Sieve set
  Soil analysis (portable field laboratory)
  Soil sample bags and boxes
  Soil hand auger
  Soil test kit (chemical)
  Soil thermometer
  Spot plate
  Water bottles

Vegetation

Specific vegetation needs include, but are not limited to:

- Manuals and handbooks on procedural guidance and other references
  - NRCS National Range and Pasture Handbook (NRPH)

- BLM Manual 4400 Rangeland Inventory, Monitoring, and Evaluation
- BLM Manual 1737-7 Procedures for Ecological Site Inventory–With Special Reference to Riparian-Wetland Sites
- National List of Plant Species That Occur in Wetlands (USFWS)
- Soil-site correlation legend
- Soil map unit descriptions

• Forms
- Vegetation Production Worksheet (Appendix 4)
- NRCS Range 417 or equivalent form

• IDSU (Inventory Data System Utilities) computer program and/or access to IDS at NSTC

• Equipment
- Rope (plots 96 ft², 0.01 acre, .01 acre)
- Planimeters (if acreages are to be compiled by field crews)

Wildlife Biology

Specific wildlife biology needs include, but are not limited to:

• Manuals and handbooks on procedural guidance and other references
- BLM Manual 6602, Integrated Habitat Inventory and Classification System (IHICS)
- Reference guides for the identification of birds, mammals, and reptiles

• Forms
- Animal Species Occurrence 6602-1
- Special Habitat Features 6602-2
- Resource Field Data Sheets 6602-3

• Computer software and documentation
- Integrated Habitat Inventory and Classification System (IHICS)

- Special Status Species Tracking (SSST)
- Species Tracking System (STS)

• Equipment
- Field glass
- Magnifying glass

Hydrology

Specific hydrology needs include, but are not limited to:

• Manuals and handbooks on procedural guidance and other references
- Stream Classification Reference (Rosgen, unpublished)
- Water Resources Council Bulletin #17B of the Hydrology Committee, "Guidelines for Determining Floodflow Frequency"
- USGS Techniques of Water-Resource Investigations Reports:
   Book 3, Chapter A1: General field and office procedures for indirect discharge measurements
   Book 3, Chapter A2: Measurement of peak discharge by the slope-area method
   Book 3, Chapter A8: Discharge measurement at gaging stations
   Book 4, Chapter A2: Frequency curves
   Book 4, Chapter B1: Low-flow investigations
- Reference guide for estimating Manning's roughness coefficient
- Reference guides for water-quality field techniques

• Computer Software and Documentation
- Statistical software, with documentation, capable of performing frequency analysis using a log-Pearson Type III frequency distribution

- Open-channel flow software, with documentation, capable of analyzing channel cross-section data, using normal depth and/or standard step calculations to produce relationships between discharge and other hydraulic parameters

• Equipment
  - Surveying equipment
      Level, rod, tripod, and survey notebook
  - Discharge measuring equipment
      Top-setting wading rod
      Current meter (Marsh-McBirney or vertical-axis current meter)
      Headset and stopwatch (if using vertical-axis current meter)
      Clipboard
      USGS discharge measurement forms

- Well points
- Water quality sampling equipment
    Thermometer
    Conductivity meter and calibration standards
    pH meter and calibration standards
    Bottles, labels, and preservatives for water samples
    Coolers with ice for sample transport to laboratory
    Field forms
    Sampling equipment for special situations
        Depth-integrating sampler (e.g., DH-48), treated for trace elements, for integrated cross-section sampling
        Bedload or bed-material sampling equipment
        Submersible, peristaltic, or other pump for shallow ground-water sampling
        Field filtration equipment for sampling dissolved chemical constituents, as opposed to sampling for total chemistry

Chapter 2 - Soils

Soil Map Unit

SOIL SURVEY INFORMATION IS IMPORTANT in mapping ecological sites and vegetation communities. One major feature of a soil survey is the soil map unit—a group of soil areas or miscellaneous areas delineated in a soil survey. Small areas of similar and dissimilar soils are classified as inclusions. Inclusions are discussed in the soil survey map unit description, but are not mapped because they are either too small to be delineated at the scale of mapping or their interpretations are similar to the dominant soil.

There are four kinds of soil map units: consociation, complex, association, and undifferentiated group. (See the National Soils Handbook (NSH), pages 627-10 and 11). The consociation map unit is the most easily understood level of mapping because only one ecological site is delineated, although mapping at such a fine detail level may not be practical due to minimum size delineations.

Consociation

A consociation is a map unit where the dominant single soil taxon or miscellaneous area makes up at least 50 percent of the area.

In a consociation, the similar soils or miscellaneous areas (soils or miscellaneous areas so similar to the dominant component that major interpretations do not significantly differ) make up less than 50 percent of the unit.

The total amount of dissimilar inclusions (soils whose interpretations differ from the dominant soil) generally does not exceed about 15 percent

if the minor components are limiting (soils whose interpretations limit the use of the soil more than the dominant soil) and 25 percent if they are nonlimiting.

Complex

A complex is a collection of two or more dissimilar kinds of soils or miscellaneous areas in a regular repeating pattern so intricate that they cannot be delineated separately due to the scale of mapping selected.

A complex consists of two or more of the following: different soils series, and/or different phases of soils series, and/or miscellaneous areas that occur in regular patterns like rock outcrops.

The total amount of dissimilar inclusions (soils whose interpretations differ from the dominant soil) generally does not exceed about 15 percent if the minor components are limiting (soils whose interpretations limit the use of the soil more than the dominant soil) and 25 percent if they are nonlimiting.

Association

An association is similar to a complex, but differs because the major soil components or miscellaneous areas occur in repeatable patterns and could have been broken out into separate soil map units at the scale of mapping but were not.

Soil association maps for low intensity land use management are more efficient and cost effective than more detailed mapping without detracting from the utility of the soil survey. It is more efficient to group and interpret several soils into one map unit rather than delineate separate map units.

The information about individual soil series are not lost, since their percentages and positions on the landscape are identified in the soil map unit description.

The total amount of dissimilar inclusions (soils whose interpretations differ from the dominant soil) generally does not exceed about 15 percent if the minor components are limiting (soils whose interpretations limit the use of the soil more than the dominant soil) and 25 percent if they are nonlimiting.

Undifferentiated Group

Undifferentiated soil groups consist of two or more taxon components that are not consistently associated geographically and therefore do not always occur together in the same map unit. These taxa are included in the same named map unit because use and management of the soils are the same or are very similar for common uses.

Every delineation in an undifferentiated group has at least one of the major components and may have all the components.

The same principles regarding the proportion of minor components that apply to consociations also apply to undifferentiated groups

Soil Map Unit Development

Soil map units are developed based on broad landscape features. These landscape features are further broken down into characteristic landforms and geomorphic components, such as hills, side slopes, toe slopes, floodplains, and depressions. The kinds of areas associated with these segments are then identified. Often, distinct vegetation patterns occur along these same landform and geomorphic surfaces. Generally, soil map units represent soil components that are repeated on the landscape.

Soil Map Unit Descriptions

Soil map unit descriptions characterize the map unit as it is identified and delineated during the soil mapping process. The contents of a map unit description will provide information to the user detailing the setting for each dominant soil component. A brief soil profile description is given that details distinctive surface features, vegetation relationships, and soil properties that affect use and management. All dissimilar soil inclusions are identified and their differences in landscape setting and soil profile characteristics are noted in the description. From these descriptions, the user should be able to determine the patterns and percent of occurrence of each component soil and soil inclusion within the map unit and their position on the landscape.

Detailed Soil Maps

Base maps of soil surveys are primarily of two kinds:

- Rectified photo base maps (high-altitude photography)

- Orthophoto base maps (high-altitude photography with the displacement of images removed).

Soil map units are delineated on the base map to provide location and spatial relationships of soils for subsequent analysis. A map unit symbol can either be numeric, alphabetic, or a combination of both (NSH, page 627-7). It consists of no more than five elements (characters), including digits, letters, and hyphens that identify the delineation. The best way to assign map unit symbols is to sequentially number them and add alpha characters to describe the slope range of the map unit. The symbol also provides the reference to a map unit description and associated information. It's possible that field map unit symbols could change at final correlation prior to the publication of the soil survey.

Soil Survey Mapping for Riparian-Wetland Areas

Most published soil survey maps, especially at the 1:24,000 scale are not detailed enough to delineate riparian-wetland areas, most streams, seeps, springs, potholes, and other small wet areas. This may necessitate delineating soil map units on a larger scale photo.

One alternative, where GIS capability is available, is to photographically or digitally enlarge an orthophoto quad base map to scales between 1:6,000 and 1:12,000 (Batson et al., 1987), delineate and identify the riparian-wetland map units, and then digitize the areas of the base maps. It is feasible to map riparian-wetland areas at a photo scale of 1:2,400 and perform a map transfer to 1:6,000 scale (a reduction of 2.5 times) if that amount of detail is needed. Riparian- wetland map unit delineations using this method would be quite small, but data entry into GIS would be possible.

A second alternative is to simply designate line segments on a scale of 1:24,000 to represent stream segments as a map unit and spot symbol map units for other kinds of riparian-wetland areas. When either line-break to line-break or dot-to-dot line segments and ad hoc or dot spot symbols are used, the average width of stream segments or the average area of spot symbols will have to be described in the map unit description. This method is used with or without GIS capability and soil survey area base maps are needed for reports. See Appendix 2, Soil Map Unit Delineations, for more details on using these techniques. Figure 2 is a schematic representation of a soil map that includes line segments. Each area with a symbol represents a soil map unit.

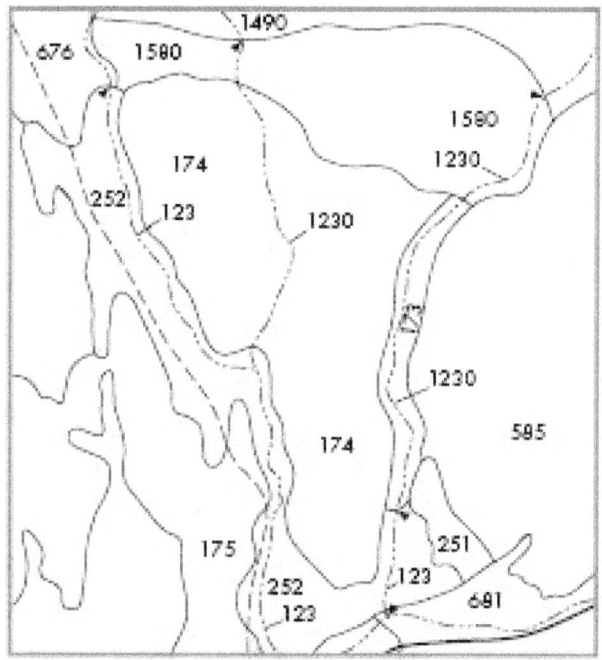

Figure 2 - Schematic Representation of Soil Map with Line Segments. Each area with a symbol represents a soil map unit.

Importance of Soil Map Units

The soil map unit provides the spatial relationship between soils or groups of soils and landscapes. The map unit also provides the link between the location of named soil taxa and tabular information on specific soil properties and interpretations for use and management.

In addition, soil map unit delineations provide the initial spatial relationship between ecological sites, which are correlated to the soil components of a map unit. Because of the relationship between landscape patterns, soils, and ecological sites, soil maps are an excellent base for other resource delineations or interpretive maps, such as wildlife habitat, recreational areas, watershed conditions, livestock utilization, and many others.

Chapter 3 - Ecological Sites

Definition of Ecological Site

RANGELAND LANDSCAPES ARE DIVIDED into ecological sites for the purposes of inventory, evaluation, and management. An ecological site is a distinctive kind of land with specific physical characteristics that differs from other kinds of land in its ability to produce a distinctive kind and amount of vegetation. It is the product of all the environmental factors responsible for its development, and it has a set of key characteristics (soils, hydrology, and vegetation) that are included in the ecological site description. Development of the soils, hydrology, and vegetation are all interrelated. Each is influenced by the other and influences the development of the others.

An ecological site has characteristic *soils* that have developed over time throughout the soil development process. The factors of soil development are parent material, climate, living organisms, topography or landscape position, and time. These factors lead to soil development or degradation through the processes of loss, addition, translocation, and transformation. Soils with like properties produce and support a distinctive kind and amount of vegetation and are grouped into the same ecological site.

An ecological site has a characteristic *hydrology*, particularly infiltration and runoff, that has developed over time. The development of the hydrology is influenced by development of the soil and plant community.

An ecological site has evolved a characteristic kind (cool season, warm season, grassland, shrub-grass, sedge meadowland) and amount of *vegetation*. The plant community on an ecological site is typified by an association of species that differs from that of other ecological sites in the kind and/or proportion of species or in annual production. These vegetation communities evolved with a characteristic kind of herbivory (kinds and numbers of herbivores, seasons of use, intensity of use) and fire regime. Fire frequency and intensity contributed to the characteristic plant community of the site.

Succession and Retrogression

Succession is the process of soil and plant community development on an ecological site. Retrogression is the change in species composition away from the historic climax plant community due to management or severe natural climatic events.

Succession occurs over time and is a result of interactions of climate, soil development, plant growth, and natural disturbances existing on the site through time. Primary succession is the formation process that begins on substrates having never previously supported any vegetation (e.g., lava flows, volcanic ash deposits). Secondary succession occurs on previously formed soil from which the vegetation has been partially or completely removed.

Ecological site development associated with climatic conditions and normal range of disturbances (e.g., occurrence of fire, grazing, unusually wet periods, flooding) produce a plant community in dynamic equilibrium with these conditions. This plant community is referred to as the historic climax plant community.

Vegetation dynamics on an ecological site includes succession and retrogression. The pathway of secondary succession is often not simply a reversal of disturbances responsible for retrogression and may not follow the same pathway as primary succession.

States and Transition Pathways

A state and transition model is used to describe vegetation dynamics and management interactions associated with each ecological site. A state and transition model provides a method to organize and communicate complex information about vegetation response to disturbances (e.g., fire, lack of fire, drought, unusually wet periods, insects, and disease) and management.

A *state* is a recognizable, relatively resistant and resilient complex with attributes that include characteristic climate, soil resource including soil biota, and the associated aboveground plant communities (Figure 3). The soil and vegetation

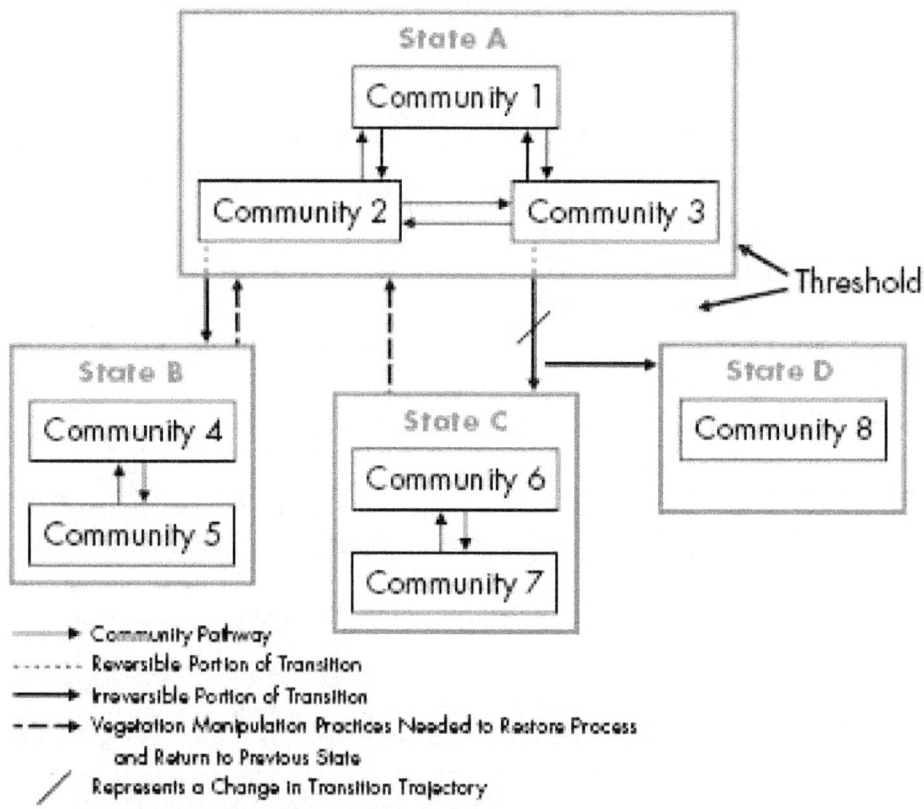

Figure 3 - State and Transition Model Diagram for an Ecological Site. (Reproduced from the NRCS National Range and Pasture Handbook, 2001.)

components are inseparably connected through ecological processes that interact to produce a sustained equilibrium that is expressed by a specific suite of plant communities. The primary ecological processes are water cycle, nutrient cycle, and the process of energy capture. Each state has distinctive characteristics, benefits, and values depending upon the intended use, products, and environmental effects desired from the site.

Two important attributes of a state are resistance and resilience. Resistance refers to the capability of the state to absorb disturbance and stresses and retain its ecological structure. Resilience refers to the amount of disturbance or stress a state can endure and still regain its original function after the disturbances and stresses are removed.

States are relatively stable and resistant to disturbances up to a threshold point. A threshold is the boundary between two states, such that one or more of the ecological processes has been irreversibly changed. Irreversible implies that restoration cannot be accomplished through natural events or a simple change in management. Active restoration (e.g., root plowing, seeding, chaining, prescribed fire, intensive grazing management) must be accomplished before a return to a previous state is possible. Additional thresholds may occur along the irreversible portion of a transition causing a change in the trajectory toward another state as illustrated in Figure 3. Once a threshold is crossed, a disequilibrium among one or more of the primary ecological processes exists and will be expressed through changes in the vegetative community and eventually the soil resource. A new stable state is formed when the system reestablishes equilibrium among its primary ecological processes.

A *transition* is the trajectory of system change between states that will not cease before the establishment of a new state. Transitions can be triggered by natural events, management actions, or both. Some transitions may occur very quickly and others over a long period of time. Two portions of a transition are recognized: reversible and irreversible. Prior to crossing a threshold, a transition is reversible and represents an opportunity to reverse or arrest the change. Vegetation manipulation practices, and if needed, facilitating practices, are used to reverse the transition. Once a threshold is crossed, the transition is irreversible without significant inputs of management resources and energy. Significant inputs are associated with accelerating practices, such as brush management and range planting.

States are not static as they encompass a certain amount of variation due to climatic events, management actions, or both. Dynamics within a state do not represent a state change since a threshold is not crossed. In order to organize information for management decisionmaking purposes, it may be desirable at times to describe these different expressions of dynamics within the states. These different vegetative assemblages within states will be referred to as plant communities and the change between these communities as community pathways.

Figure 3 illustrates the different components of a state and transition model diagram for an ecological site. States are represented by the large boxes and are bordered by thresholds. The small boxes represent plant communities with community pathways representing the cause of change between communities. The entire trajectory from one state to another state is considered a transition (i.e., from State A to State B). The portion of the transition contained within the boundary of a state is considered reversible with a minimum of input from management. Once the transition has crossed the threshold, it is not reversible without substantial input (vegetation manipulation practices). The arrow returning to a previous state (State B to State A) will be utilized to designate types of practices needed. Additional thresholds occurring along a transition may change the trajectory of a transition (from State C to State D).

The first vegetation state described in an ecological site description is the historic climax plant community or naturalized plant community (Community 1 from Figure 3). From this state, a "road map" to other states has been developed. Each transition will be identified separately and described, incorporating as much information known concerning the causes of change, changes in ecological processes, and any known probabilities associated with the transitions. Plant communities and community pathways within states may be described as needed.

Historic Climax Plant Community

The historic climax plant community for an ecological site is the plant community that existed before European immigration and settlement. This plant community was best adapted to the unique combination of environmental factors associated with the site. The historic climax plant community was in dynamic equilibrium with its environment. It is the plant community that was able to avoid displacement by the suite of disturbances and disturbance patterns (i.e., magnitude and frequency) that naturally occurred within the area occupied by the site. Natural disturbances, such as drought, fire, unusually wet periods, and grazing (e.g., native

fauna and insects) were inherent in the development and maintenance of these plant communities. The effects of these disturbances are part of the range of characteristics of the site that contribute to that dynamic equilibrium. Fluctuations in plant community structure and function caused by the effects of these natural disturbances establish the boundaries of dynamic equilibrium. They are accounted for as part of the range of characteristics for an ecological site. Some sites may have a small range of variation, while others have a large range. Plant communities that are subjected to abnormal disturbances and physical site deterioration or that are protected from natural influences, such as fire and grazing, for long periods seldom typify the historic climax plant community.

The historic climax plant community of an ecological site is not a precise assemblage of species for which the proportions are the same from place to place or from year to year. In all plant communities, variability is apparent in productivity and occurrence of individual species. Spatial boundaries of the communities, however, can be recognized by characteristic patterns of species composition and community structure.

Naturalized Plant Community

Ecological site descriptions have been developed for all identified ecological sites. In some parts of the country, however, the historic climax plant community has been destroyed, and it is impossible to reconstruct that plant community with any degree of reliability. In these regions, site descriptions have been developed using the naturalized plant communities for the site. The use of this option for ecological site descriptions is limited to those sites where the historic climax plant community has been destroyed and cannot be reconstructed with any degree of reliability. The annual grasslands of California are an example of a naturalized plant community.

Potential Natural Community

A potential natural community (PNC) is defined as the biotic community that would become established on an ecological site if all successional sequences were completed without interference by people under the present environmental conditions. The term "potential natural community" was recommended for use by the Range Inventory Standardization Committee (RISC) in its 1983 report to replace the term "historic climax plant community." The RISC report's rationale was that PNC recognizes past influences by man, including past use and introduced exotic species of animals or plants. Man's influence is excluded from the present onward to eliminate the complexities of management. The concepts of climax and PNC both refer to a relatively stable community resulting from secondary succession after disturbance. Although man may or may not have caused the disturbance, succession to climax or PNC occurs without further perceptible influences of man's activity. PNC is the preferred term because it explicitly recognizes that naturalized exotic species may persist in the final stage of secondary succession and that succession after disturbance does not always reestablish the original vegetation.

Historic Climax Plant Community Versus Potential Natural Community

In this document, the term "historic climax plant community" is used in reference to the official ecological site description. NRCS still requires the documentation of a historic climax plant community in the revision or preparation of new site descriptions. BLM managers and resource personal have the option of using a PNC for evaluation of similarity indices rather than an historic climax plant community. In order to use PNC there must be compelling evidence that a particular species or group of species, not included in the historic climax plant community, should be included in more advanced successional vegetation communities.

Changes in Ecological Site Potential

Severe physical deterioration of an ecological site can permanently alter the potential to support the original plant community. Examples include permanently lowering the water table, severe surface drainage caused by gullying, and severe soil erosion. When the ecological site's potential has significantly changed, it is no longer considered the same site. A change to another ecological site is then recognized, and a new site description may need to be developed on the basis of its altered potential.

Some ecological sites have been invaded by or planted to introduced species. The introduced species may become well established or naturalized to the site. They may dominate the site, or they may continue to occupy part of the site even when secondary succession has restored the plant community to near historic climax conditions. In these cases of invasion or introduction of nonnative species, a change in ecological site is not recognized because the edaphic and climatic potential for the site has not been altered.

Characteristic Vegetation States of an Ecological Site

Where possible, the historic climax plant community for each ecological site has been determined. Where it is not possible to determine the historic climax plant community, the naturalized plant community will be described. In addition to the historic climax plant community or naturalized plant community, other plant communities that comprise the known steady states of vegetation will be determined and included in future ecological site descriptions.

The description of each plant community should have been considered as an approximation subject to modification as additional knowledge becomes available.

Characteristics of a plant community obtained from several sources or sites should have been used to describe the plant communities. The following factors have been considered in evaluating plant information:

- Effects of fire or lack of fire
- Impacts of grazing or lack of grazing
- Impacts of rodent concentrations
- Impacts from insects
- Soil erosion or deposition by wind or water
- Drought or unusually wet years
- Variations in hydrology and storm events
- Plant disease
- Introduced plant species

The NRCS' Ecological Site Information System (ESIS) can provide useful data in identifying plant communities. This system can be found on the World Wide Web at *http://plants.usda.gov/esis*.

Differentiation Between Ecological Sites

The following guidelines are used to differentiate one ecological site from another:

- Significant differences in the species or species groups that are in the historic climax plant community, such as the presence (or absence) of one or more species that make up 10 percent or more of the historic climax plant community by air-dry weight (ADW)

- Significant differences in the relative proportion of species or species groups in the historic climax plant community, such as a 20 percent (absolute) change in composition by ADW between any two species in the historic climax plant community

- Significant differences in the total annual production in the historic climax plant community

- Soil factor differences that determine plant production and composition, the hydrology of the site, and the functioning of the ecological processes of the water cycle, nutrient cycles, and energy flow

Any differences in these guidelines (either singly or in combination) great enough to indicate a different use potential or to require different management, are the basis for establishing or differentiating a site.

These guidelines are not definitive for site differentiation or combination. The differences between sites may be finer or broader than the guidelines. Rationale, and the site features listed in the respective ecological site descriptions, should readily and consistently distinguish the differences.

Differences in kind, proportion, or production of species are the result of differences in soil, topography, climate, and other environmental factors. Slight variations in these factors are not criteria for site differentiation; however, individual environmental factors are frequently associated with significant differences in historic climax plant communities. The presence or absence of a water table within the root zone of highly saline soil in contrast to a nonsaline soil is dramatically reflected in plant communities that such soils support. Marked changes in soil texture, depth, and topographic position usually result in pronounced differences in plant communities, total production, or both. Therefore, such contrasting conditions in the soil characteristics, climate, topography, and other environmental factors known to be associated with a specific ecological site can be used as a means of identifying the site when the historic climax plant community is absent.

Generally, one species or group of species dominate a site. Dominant status does not vary from year to year. Because of their stability in the historic climax plant community, dominant species have often been used to distinguish sites and to differentiate one site from another.

In evaluating the significance of kinds, proportion, and production of species or species groups that are dominant in a historic climax plant community, and given different soil characteristics, the relative proportion of species may indicate whether one or more ecological sites are involved. For example, in one area the historic climax plant community may consist of 60 percent big bluestem and 10 percent little bluestem, and in another area it may consist of 60 percent little bluestem and 10 percent big bluestem. Thus, two ecological sites are recognized. Even though the production and species are similar, the

proportion's difference distinguishes them as separate sites.

The effect of any single environmental factor can vary, depending on the influence of other factors. For example, soil depth is more significant on a site that receives extra water from runoff or in a high precipitation zone than on an upland site in a low precipitation area. An additional 2 inches of annual rainfall may be highly important in a section of the country that has an arid climate, but of minor significance in a humid climate. A difference in average annual production of 100 pounds per acre, ADW, is of minor importance on ecological sites capable of producing 2,000 pounds per acre. This difference, however, is highly significant on sites capable of producing only 200 to 300 pounds per acre. Similar variations in degree of significance apply to most factors of the environment. Consequently, in the identification of an ecological site, consideration was given to its environment as a whole, as well as to the individual components.

Where changes in soils, aspect, topography, or moisture conditions are abrupt, ecological site boundaries are distinct. Boundaries are broader and less distinct where plant communities change gradually along broad environmental gradients of relatively uniform soils and topography. Making distinctions between ecological sites along a continuum is difficult. Thus, the need for site differentiation may not be readily apparent until the cumulative impact of soil and climatic differences on vegetation is examined over a broad area.

At times, less frequently occurring plants may increase on a site or the site may be invaded by plants not formerly found in the historic climax plant community. The presence or absence of these plants may fluctuate greatly because of differences in microenvironment, weather conditions, or human actions. Consequently, using them for site identification can be misleading, so they should not be used to differentiate sites. Site differentiation, characterization, and determination are based on the plant community that develops along with the soils. A study of several locations over several years is needed to differentiate and characterize a site.

Availability and accessibility to domestic livestock grazing are not factors in ecological site determination and differentiation. Site differentiation is based on those soil characteristics, response to disturbance, and environmental factors that have direct effect on the nature of the historic climax plant community production.

Revising Ecological Site Descriptions

Analysis and interpretation of new information about the soil, vegetation, and other onsite environmental factors may reveal a need to revise or update ecological site descriptions. Because the collection of such information through resource inventories and monitoring is a continuous process, site descriptions may be reviewed periodically for needed revision. It is especially important that site descriptions be reviewed when new data on production or response to disturbance become available. Documented production data, along with related soil, climate, and physiographic data, will be the basis of the site description revisions or new site descriptions.

Developing New Ecological Site Descriptions

A new ecological site description should be prepared when data analysis or new information reveals that a different or new ecological site exists. Generally, enough land area must be identified to be of importance in the management or study of the site before a new site will be developed and described. A new ecological site may be differentiated from an existing site when sufficient erosion or other action has occurred to significantly alter the site's potential.

BLM Procedures

BLM has the capability to develop new site descriptions and propose revisions to existing ecological site descriptions. However, each new site description or proposed change must be prepared using the procedure identified in Chapter 3 of the NRCS National Range and Pasture Handbook. All new and proposed revisions must be reviewed and approved by the local and State NRCS offices.

Naming Ecological Sites on Rangeland

Ecological sites have been named to help users recognize the kinds of rangeland in their locality. Names of ecological sites are brief and are based on readily recognized permanent physical features such as the kinds of soil, climate, topography, or a combination of these features. Examples of ecological site names based on these criteria are Deep Sand, Sandy, Sandy Plains, Limestone Hills,

Clay Upland, Saline Lowland, Gravely Outwash, Level Winding Riparian, Pumice Hills, Sub-irrigated, Wet Meadows, Fresh Marsh, and Sandy Savanna. Some States have chosen to add the dominant species commonly found on the site to the ecological site name. Examples are Alkali Bottom (Alkali Sacaton), Desert Clay (Shadscale), and Upland Loam (Basin Big Sagebrush).

Ecological sites having similar soils and topography may exhibit significant differences in their historic climax plant communities because of climatic differences. For example, the average annual precipitation of a clay loam in southern Arizona ranges from 12 to 16 inches. Quantitative evaluation indicates that the amount of vegetation produced in areas where precipitation is 16 to 19 inches is significantly more than that produced in areas where precipitation is 12 to 16 inches. Thus, two ecological sites are recognized and are distinguished by the inclusion of the precipitation zone (PZ) in the name of the sites, as in Clay Loam Ecological Site 12-16 PZ and Clay Loam Ecological Site 16-19 PZ.

The limited number of permanent physiographic features or other features used in naming ecological sites makes repeated use of these terms inevitable. Deep sands, for example, occur in areas of widely divergent climate and support different natural plant communities. The name Deep Sand is appropriate for each of these areas, but obviously it is used throughout the country to designate several ecological sites. Where this occurs within a land resource area, the applicable precipitation zone or other differentiating factors are to be included as part of the name. Sites that have the same name, but are in different major land resource areas, are different sites.

Numbering Ecological Sites

The ecological site number for rangelands consists of five parts:

1. The first character designates whether the site is a rangeland site (R) or a forest site (F). Since this identifier is not actually a part of the number, it is rarely used.

2. A three-digit number and one-digit letter representing the Major Land Resource Area (MLRA)

3. A single letter representing a Major Land Resource Unit (MLRU)

4. A three-digit site number assigned by the State

5. A two-digit letter State postal code

If the MLRA has only two numbers, a zero is inserted in the first space followed by the two numbers. The first letter (e.g., A, B, C) following the MLRA number represents the MLRA subdivisions. Where no MLRA subdivisions are identified, an X is used in the fourth space to denote that there is no MLRA subdivision. The fifth space is reserved for the MLRU letter for States that use the MLRU designation. For those States that do not use the MLRU designation, a Y is inserted. The next three digits represent the individual ecological site number and are assigned by the State. The final two letters are the State's two-letter postal code. An example of an ecological site number is: RO41XC313AZ

Ecological sites for MLRAs that extend into adjoining States would retain the same identification number including the State designation for both States. The State postal code attached would be the State that first described the site.

Site descriptions will be labeled as "draft" until the NRCS's State range conservationist approves the site description.

Correlating Ecological Sites

Ecological sites should have been correlated between areas, States, and MLRAs on the basis of soils, proportion of species, and annual production of the potential plant communities. In this process, ecological site descriptions are reviewed to ensure consistency in identifying and describing the same site across State, area, and MLRA boundaries. These reviews include comparing similar sites to determine whether they are in fact different ecological sites. Correlation also involves the review of soils information to ensure the description matches the soil properties in the individual soil series.

Only one name should have been given to a single site that occurs in adjacent States within the same MLRA.

Ecological Site Description

A description has been prepared for each ecological site (see an example in Appendix 3). The description identifies the important resources for the site that are used to identify, evaluate, plan, develop, manage, and monitor rangelands. The description includes the following information, as appropriate:

Heading

All ecological site descriptions will identify the USDA and Natural Resources Conservation Service.

Ecological Site Name

The full name of the site should appear on each page of the description.

Ecological Site ID

The site number is a 10-digit number that also appears on each page of the description.

Major Land Resource Area

Identifies the major land resource area code and common name.

Interstate Correlation

Lists the States that have correlated the site.

Physiographic Features

Describes the occurrence of the site on the landscape. In reference to the historic climax plant community, includes information on whether the site typically generates runoff, receives runoff from other sites, or receives and generates runoff. Physiographic features include:

- Landform
- Aspect
- Site elevation

- Slope
- Water table
- Flooding
- Ponding
- Runoff class

Climatic Features

Climatic features include:

- Frost-free period (length and dates)
- Freeze-free period (length and dates)
- Mean annual precipitation
- Monthly moisture and temperature distribution
- Location of climate stations

Influencing Water Features

Includes information regarding water features where the plant community is influenced by water or the water table from a wetland or stream associated with the site. Water features include the Cowardin wetland classification system and Rosgen stream classification system.

Representative Soil Features

The main soil properties associated with the site are briefly described. This includes:

- Properties that significantly affect plant, soil, and water relationships, and the site hydrology
- The extent of flow patterns, and the rills and gullies found in the historic climax plant community
- The amount and patterns of pedestaling and terracettes caused by wind or water inherent to the historic climax plant community

- The size and frequency of wind-scoured areas
- The susceptibility of the site to compaction
- A description of the expected organic layer and physical and chemical crusts that might be present

Representative soil features include:

- Parent materials
- Surface texture
- Subsurface texture
- Surface fragments
- Subsurface fragments
- Drainage class
- Permeability class
- Depth
- Electrical conductivity
- Sodium absorption ratio
- Calcium carbonate equivalent
- Soil reaction
- Available water holding capacity

Ecological Dynamics of the Site

The general ecological dynamics of the site are described. Included are the expected changes that are likely to occur because of variations in the weather and the effects this might have on the dynamics of the site. Included are assumptions regarding site development (e.g., fire frequency, native herbivory).

Plant Communities

This section describes:

- Vegetation dynamics of the site
- State and transition model diagram
- Common states that occur on the site and the

transitions between states. Included are the plant communities and community pathways within each state.

- Ground cover and structure
- Annual production
- Growth curves
- Photos of each state or community

The first plant community to be described should be the interpretative community. This plant community will be either the historic climax plant community or, where applicable, the naturalized plant community for the site.

Other states and plant communities that may exist on the site are also described. One or more plant communities for each state will be described. Included is a narrative describing the dynamics of each state and plant community and the causes of community pathway changes. Also described are the thresholds between states, and information that will aid in the identification and evaluation of how the ecological processes of the site are functioning.

Information regarding transitions between states should have been included in the plant community narrative, as well as causes of change and any known probabilities associated with the transitions.

Species List

A detailed species list will be included for the historic climax plant community and each stable state plant community known to exist on the site. Each listing should include the major plant species (i.e., common name and scientific name) and their normal relative production expressed in pounds ADW (pounds per acre per year) in the total plant community. Species should be listed

by life form and group, including pounds per acre allowable for each group.

Plant Groups

Ecological site descriptions usually list plant species by groups. Plant groups include:

- Cool season tall grasses
- Cool season midgrasses
- Warm season tall grasses
- Warm season midgrasses
- Warm season short grasses
- Annual grasses
- Perennial forbs
- Biennial forbs
- Annual forbs
- Succulent forbs
- Leafy forbs
- Shrubs
- Half-shrubs
- Deciduous trees
- Evergreen trees
- Cacti
- Yucca
- Yucca-like plants

Other factors used to identify groups include:

- Kind of plant
- Structure
- Size
- Rooting structure
- Life cycle
- Production
- Niche occupied
- Photosynthetic pathways

If plant groups are shown, plant groupings will identify whether individual species within the group have a production limitation or whether a single species can account for the entire group allowable.

Groups may be subdivided into separate groups or combined. For instance, two or three groups of warm season mid-grasses may be described because of different niches occupied and differences in production, structure, elevation, and climatic adaptations in the area of the site.

Cover and Structure

The following table (Table 3) is an adaptation of the table on ground cover and structure found in Appendix 3. Table 3 has been changed to more

clearly illustrate ground cover and canopy cover layers (structure) for use by BLM.

Ground cover is the percentage of material, other than bare ground, that protects the soil surface from being hit directly by a raindrop. This would include first contact with plant canopy cover, biological crust, litter, rock fragments, bedrock, and water.

Canopy cover is the percentage of ground covered by a vertical projection of the outermost perimeter of the natural spread of foliage of plants.

Structure is the average height and canopy cover of each layer of vegetation.

Table 3 - Cover and Structure

	Ground and Canopy Cover									
	Structure - Height Above the Ground									
	Not Applicable		6–12 inches		12–24 inches		24–60 inches		180–240 inches	
	%ground cover	%canopy cover	%ground cover	%canopy cover	%ground cover	%canopy cover	%ground cover	%canopy cover	%ground cover	%canopy cover
Trees										
Shrubs										
Forbs										
Grasses										
Litter										
Cryptogams										
Rock Fragments										
Bare Ground										

Biological Soil Crust Communities

Information on biological soil crust communities (e.g., mosses, lichens, cyanobacteria, algae) usually includes only cover data. However, on tundra sites where current production can be determined on lichens and mosses, production may be expressed as total live biomass.

Total Annual Production

Total annual production is shown as the median air-dry production and the fluctuations to be expected during favorable, normal, and unfavorable years. In areas where examples of the historic climax plant community are not available, the highest production in plant communities for which examples are available have been used.

Plant Community Growth Curves

Plant community growth curves are displayed for each important plant community. Growth curves indicate the percent of growth by month (Table 4). This includes:

• **Number** - This number is used only one time in each State. The first 2 digits are the State postal code, and the last 4 digits are consecutive numbers from 001 to 9999.
• **Name** - This is a brief descriptive name for each curve.

If plant community growth curves are not available, contact the NRCS.

Table 4 - Plant Community Growth Curves

Growth curve number:
Growth curve name:
Growth curve description:

Jan	Feb	March	April	May	June	July	Aug.	Sept.	Oct.	Nov.	Dec.

Ecological Site Interpretations

This section includes the site interpretations for the use and management of the site. The information includes:

Animal Community
This narrative describes the major wildlife species that occupy or use the site. It will include any major values or problems associated with their use of this site and the plant communities that may occur on it. Special status animal species, such as threatened and endangered species, and State or local species of concern are discussed. General descriptions of the use of this site by livestock and wild horses and burros should also be included. Suitability of the site for grazing by season and by kind and class of

livestock will be addressed. Included in the discussion is a list of major barriers to wildlife and livestock use (e.g., water, topography).

Hydrologic Functions

This discussion includes effects on the hydrologic functions from shifts to different plant communities. There should be a description of the changes in infiltration and runoff characteristics expected due to changes in plant communities and soil surface characteristics. Information about water budgets for each plant community could be included.

Recreational Uses

Potential recreational uses that the site can support or that may influence the management of the site should be discussed. Included will be a list of special concerns that affect the maintenance of the recreational potentials or site conditions that may limit its potential. Also listed are plant species that have special aesthetic values, uses, and landscape value.

Wood Products

Indicates use or potential uses of significant species that may influence the management of the site.

Other Products

Indicates the use or potential uses of other products produced on the site. These may include landscape plants, nuts, berries, mushrooms, and biomass for energy potentials.

Supporting Information

This narrative involves information about the relationship of this site to other ecological sites. Includes information regarding documentation and references used to develop the ecological site description.

Associated Sites

This is a listing and description of other ecological sites that are commonly located in conjunction with this site.

Similar Sites

Identifies and describes ecological sites that resemble or can be confused with the site.

Inventory Data References

Includes a listing of sample transects or plots supporting the site description.

State Correlation

Includes the states that this site has been correlated with.

Type Locality

Includes the location of a typical example of the site. Indicates township, range, and section or longitude and latitude of the specific location.

Relationship to Other Established Classification Systems

Includes a description of how this ecological site description may relate to other established classification systems.

Other References

Includes other reference information used in site development or in understanding the ecological dynamics of the site.

Ecological Site Documentation and References

Each ecological site description documents the following information about the preparation of the original or latest version of the description:

Authorship

The original author's initials and date. Revision author's initials and revision date.

Site Approval

Includes signature, title, and date of the State technical specialist who reviewed and approved the ecological site description.

Forestland Ecological Sites

Forestland ecological site descriptions normally characterize the mature forest plant community that historically occupied the site as well as the other major plant communities that commonly occupy the site. An example of a forestland ecological site description can be found in the NRCS National Forestry Manual, part 537, subpart E, exhibit 537-14.

Separating Forested Lands from Rangelands in Areas Where They Interface

Rangeland and forested land ecological sites are separated based on the historic kind of vegetation that occupied the site. Forested land ecological sites are assigned and described where this historic vegetation was dominated by trees. Rangeland ecological sites are assigned where overstory tree production was not dominant in the climax vegetation.

Chapter 4 - Production Data

Aboveground Vegetation Production

ALL PRODUCTION AND COMPOSITION data collected are based on weight measurements. Weight is the most meaningful expression of the productivity of a plant community or an individual species.

Production is determined by measuring the annual aboveground growth of vegetation. Some aboveground growth is used by insects and rodents, or it disappears because of weathering before production measurements are made. Therefore, these determinations represent a productivity index. They are valuable for comparing the production of different rangeland ecological sites, plant species composition, and similarity index.

Comprehensive interpretation of plant production and composition requires that data be representative of all species having measurable production. Rangeland and other grazing lands may be used or have potential for use by livestock and wildlife, as recreation areas, as a source of certain wood products, for scenic viewing, and for other soil and water conservation purposes. The value of plant species for domestic livestock often is not the same as that for wildlife, recreation, beautification, and watershed protection. Furthermore, the principles and concepts of rangeland ecological site, similarity index, and other interpretations are based on the total plant community. Therefore, interpretations of a plant community are not limited solely to species that have value for domestic livestock.

The procedures and techniques discussed in this section relate primarily to rangeland. Most of them, however, also apply to grazeable forest and native or naturalized pasture. Changes or modifications in procedures required for land other than rangeland are described.

Total Annual Production

The total aboveground production of all plant species of a plant community during a single year is total annual production. Total annual production includes the aboveground parts of all plants produced during a single growth year, regardless of accessibility to grazing animals. An increase in the stem diameter of trees and shrubs, production from previous years, and underground growth are excluded.

Production for Various Kinds of Plants

The Vegetation Production Worksheet (Appendix 4) can be used to record production data on individual plots.

Herbaceous Plants

These plants include grasses (except bamboos), grasslike plants, and forbs. Annual production includes all aboveground growth of leaves, stems, inflorescence, and fruits produced in a single year.

Woody Plants

Determining production of trees and large shrubs by harvesting portions of stands is time consuming and impractical. Research scientists are devising methods for calculating current production of some species on the basis of measurements of such factors as crown width or height and basal area. These data are helpful in estimating the annual production of trees and large shrubs. (Appendix 5 provides an example of estimating annual production on Utah Juniper.)

Deciduous Trees, Shrubs, Half-shrubs, and Woody Vines

Annual production includes leaves, current twigs, inflorescence, vine elongation, and fruits produced in a single year.

Evergreen Trees, Shrubs, Half-shrubs, and Woody Vines

Annual production includes current year leaves (or needles), current twigs, inflorescence, vine elongation, and fruits produced in a single year.

Yucca, Agave, Nolina, Sotol, and Saw Palmetto

Annual production consists of new leaves, the amount of enlargement of old leaves, and fruiting stem and fruit produced in a single year. Until more specific data are available and if current growth is not readily distinguishable, consider annual production as 15 percent of the total green- leaf weight plus the weight of current fruiting stems and fruit. Adjust this percentage in years of obviously high or low production.

Cacti

Prickly Pear and Other Pad-forming Cacti

Annual production consists of pads, fruit, and spines produced in a single year plus enlargement of old pads in that year. Until more specific data are available and if current growth is not readily distinguishable, consider annual production as 10 percent of the total weight of pads plus current fruit production. Adjust this percentage for years of obviously high or low production.

Barrel-type Cactus

Until specific data are available, consider annual production as 5 percent of the total weight of the plant, other than fruit, plus the weight of fruit produced in a single year.

Cholla-type Cactus

Until specific data are available and if current growth is not readily distinguishable, consider annual production as 15 percent of the total weight of photosynthetically active tissue plus the weight of fruit produced in a single year.

Methods of Determining Production

Production of a plant community can be determined by estimating, by harvesting, or by a combination of estimating and harvesting (double sampling) depending on the intended use of the data.

Some plants are on State lists of threatened or endangered species, or are otherwise protected species. Regulations concerning these species may conflict with the harvesting procedures described. For example, barrel-type cactus in some States is a protected species, and harvesting is not allowed.

The weight of such plants is to be estimated unless special permission for harvesting can be obtained. Examiners determining production should be aware of such plant lists and regulations.

When estimating or harvesting plants, include all parts of all plants within the plot, and exclude all portions outside the plot, even though the plants are rooted within the plot. Include portions of plants extending into the plot, but rooted outside the plot (Figure 4).

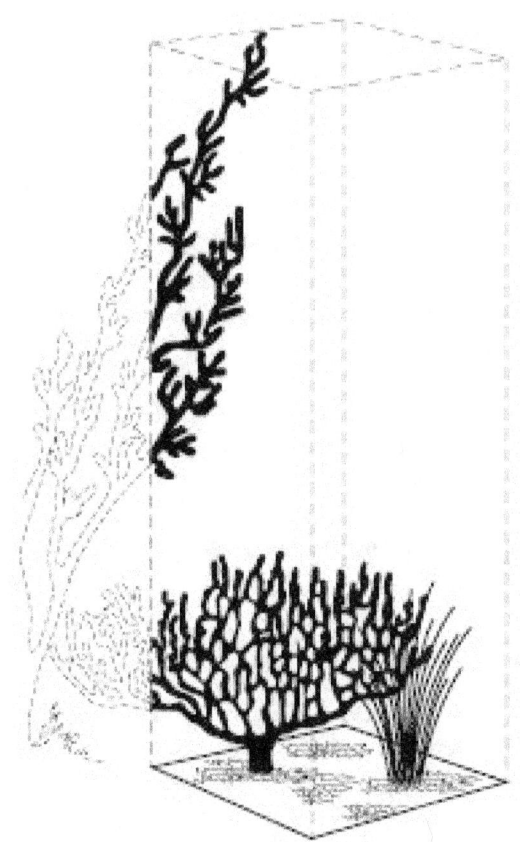

Exclude
all parts of
all plants
outside the plot

Include
all parts of
all plants
within the plot

Figure 4 - Weight Estimate Plots.
(Adapted from Sampling Vegetation
Attributes, Technical Reference 1734-4,
Illustration 23, 1996.)

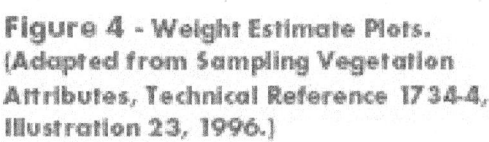

Estimating by Weight Units

The relationship of weight to volume is not constant; therefore, production and composition determinations are based on weight estimates, not on comparison of relative volumes. The weight unit method is an efficient means of estimating production and lends itself readily to self-training. This method is based on the following:

- A weight unit is established for each plant species occurring on the area being examined.

- A weight unit can consist of part of a plant, an entire plant, or a group of plants (see Appendix 6, Examples of Weight Units).

- The size and weight of a unit vary according to the kind of plant. For example, a unit of 5 to 10 grams is suitable for small grass or forb species. Weight units for large plants may be several pounds or kilograms.

- If a majority of estimates for a particular species are in fractions of a weight unit (e.g., 0.1, 0.5, 0.7), then the size of the weight unit is probably too high.

- Other considerations include:
  - Length, width, thickness, and number of stems and leaves
  - Ratio of leaves to stems
  - Growth form and relative compactness of species

The following procedure can be used to establish a weight unit for a species:

1. Decide on a weight unit (in pounds or grams) that is appropriate for the species.

2. Visually select part of a plant, an entire plant, or a group of plants that will most likely equal this weight.

3. Harvest and weigh the plant material to determine actual weight.

4. Repeat this process until the desired weight unit can be estimated with reasonable accuracy.

5. Maintain proficiency in estimating by periodically harvesting and weighing to check estimates of production.

The procedure for estimating production and composition of a single plot is:

1. Estimate species composition by visually estimating the percent by weight of each species with the total weight for the entire plot.

2. Estimate production by counting the weight units of each species in the plot.

3. Convert weight units for each species to grams or pounds.

4. Harvest and weigh each species to check estimates of production.

5. Compute composition on the basis of actual weights to check composition estimates.

6. Repeat the process until proficiency in estimating is attained.

7. Periodically repeat the process to maintain proficiency in estimating.

8. Keep the harvested materials, when necessary, for air-drying and weighing to convert from field (green) weight to air-dry weight (ADW).

Double Sampling—Estimating and Harvesting

The double-sampling method is to be used in making most production and similarity index determinations. The procedure is:

1. Select a study area consisting of one soil taxonomic unit. This should be a soil taxonomic unit that is an important component of a rangeland ecological site or forestland ecological site.

2. Select plots at specified intervals along a linear transect. The starting point is randomly located within the site write-up area (SWA).

3. After plots are selected, estimate and record the weight of each species in each plot using the weight-unit method. When estimating or harvesting, include all parts of all plants within the plot. Exclude all portions of all plants outside the vertical projection of the plot.

4. After weights have been estimated on all plots, select the plots to be harvested. The plots selected should include all or most of the species in the estimated plots. If an important species occurs on some of the estimated plots, but not on the harvested plots, it can be clipped individually on one or more plots. The number of plots harvested depends on the number estimated. To adequately correct the estimates, research indicates at

least one plot should be harvested for each seven estimated. At least 2 plots are to be harvested if 10 are estimated, and 3 are to be harvested if 20 are estimated. Table 5 shows the minimum number of plots to be harvested based on the number of estimated plots.

Table 5 - Number of Harvested Plots

Number of Plots Estimated	Minimum Number of Harvested Plots
1 - 7	1
8 - 14	2
15 - 21	3
22 - 28	4
29 - 35	5
36 - 42	6

5. Harvest, weigh, and record the weight of each species in the plots selected for harvesting. Harvest all parts of all plants within the plot. Exclude all portions of all plants outside the vertical projection of the plot.

Correct estimated weights by calculating an adjustment factor. To do this, divide the harvested weight of each species by the estimated weight for the corresponding species on the harvested plots. This factor is used to correct the estimates for that species in each plot. A factor of more than 1.0 indicates the estimate is too low. A factor lower than 1.0 indicates the estimate is too high.

6. After plots are estimated and harvested and adjustment factors for estimates computed, air-dry percentages are determined by air-drying the harvested materials or by selecting

the appropriate factor from an air-dry percentage table (Appendix 7). Values for each species are then corrected to air-dry pounds per acre or kilograms per hectare for all plots. Average weight and percentage composition can then be computed for the sample area.

Plot Size

Adapt the size and shape of plots to the kind of plants to be sampled. The area of a plot can be expressed in square feet, inches and meters, or in acres.

If vegetation is relatively short, the following plot sizes work best in determining production:

0.96 ft² or 41.7 inch circumference
1.92 ft² or 59 inch circumference
2.40 ft² or 66 inch circumference
4.80 ft² or 93.2 inch circumference
9.60 ft² or 131.8 inch circumference

The listed plots are the most useful when converting grams to pounds per acre. The 9.6 ft² plot is generally used in areas where vegetation density and production are relatively light. The smaller plots, especially the 0.96 ft² and 1.92 ft² plots, are satisfactory in areas of homogeneous, relatively dense vegetation like that occurring in meadows. Plots larger than 9.6 ft² should be used where vegetation is very sparse and heterogeneous.

If the vegetation consists of trees or large shrubs, larger plots must be used. If the tree or shrub population is uniform, a 0.01 acre plot is more suitable. If vegetation is unevenly spaced, a more accurate sample can be obtained by using a 0.1 acre plot, 4.356 feet wide and 1,000 feet long. For statistical analyses, 10 plots of 0.01 acre are superior to a single 0.1 acre plot. Plots of 0.1 and

0.01 acre are most useful when production data is collected in pounds because it is a direct conversion.

If vegetation is mixed, two sizes of plots generally are needed. A series of 10 square or rectangular plots of 0.01 acre and a smaller plot, such as the 9.6-square-foot plot nested in a designated corner of each larger plot, is suitable. The 0.01-acre plot is used for trees or large shrubs, and the smaller plot for lower-growing plants. Weights of the vegetation from both plots are then converted to pounds per acre. Plots with area expressed in square meters are used if production is to be determined in kilograms per hectare.

If the plots are nested, production from both plots must be recorded in the same units of measure. For example, a plot 20 meters by 20 meters (or other dimensions that equal 400 meters) can be used for measuring the tree and shrub vegetation and a 1-meter plot nested in a designated corner can be used for measuring the low-growing plants. Determine the production from both in grams and convert the grams to kilograms per hectare. Plots of 0.25, 1, 10, 100, and 400 square meters are commonly used.

Plot Shape

Plots can be circular, square, or rectangular. However, long-narrow plots are likely to be more accurate than circular, square, or rectangular plots (Krebs 1989). Edge effect can result in significant measurement bias if the plots are too small (Wiegert 1962). Since aboveground vegetation must be clipped in some plots, circular plots should be avoided because of the difficulty in cutting around the perimeter of the circle with hand shears and the likely measurement bias that would result.

Harvesting

This method is similar to the double-sampling method except that all plants in all plots are harvested. The double-sampling procedures for estimating weight by species and the subsequent correction of estimates do not apply. Conversion of harvested weight to air-dry pounds per acre or kilograms per hectare are performed according to the procedures described for double sampling.

Units of Production and Conversion Factors

All production data are to be expressed as ADW in pounds per acre (lb/acre) or in kilograms per hectare (kg/ha). The field weight must be converted to ADW. This may require drying or the use of locally developed conversion tables.

Plot Size Conversion Factors

All weights need to be converted to pounds per acre. The following plot size conversion factors (CFs) calculate pound per acre or kilograms per hectare for various weight units (e.g., grams or pounds) and plot sizes (e.g., 9.6 ft², 0.1 acre, 1 m², 400 m²).

The weight of vegetation on plots measured in square feet or in acres can be estimated and harvested in grams or in pounds, but weight is generally expressed in grams. If weights are collected on 10 plots, the total weight is converted to pounds per acre by using the factor in column 3. If production is collected on less (or more) then 10 plots, divide the total for the entire transect by the number of plots and use the conversion factor in column 4.

To convert grams to pounds per acre, use the conversions in Table 6.

Table 6 - Conversion Factors for Grams to Pounds per Acre

Plot Size	Weight Unit	Conversion Factor Per 10 Plots	Conversion Factor Per Plot
0.96 ft²	grams	10	100
1.92 ft²	grams	5	50
2.4 ft²	grams	4	40
4.8 ft²	grams	2	20
9.6 ft²	grams	1	10
96. ft²	grams	0.1	1
.01 acre	grams	10	100
.1 acre	grams	1	10

In the metric system, a square-meter plot (or multiple thereof) is used. Weight on these plots is estimated or harvested in grams and converted to kilograms per hectare. A hectare equals 10,000 square meters. A kilogram equals 1,000 grams. If weights are collected on 10 plots, the total weight is converted to kilograms per hectare by using the factor in column 3. If production is collected on less (or more) then 10 plots, divide the total for the entire transect by the number of plots and use the conversion factor in column 4.

To convert grams per plot to kilograms per hectare, use the conversions in Table 7.

Table 7 - Conversion Factors for Grams to Kilograms per Hectare

Plot Size	Weight Unit	Conversion Factor Per 10 Plots	Conversion Factor Per Plot
0.25 m²	grams	10	100
1 m²	grams	10	100
10 m²	grams	10	100
100 m²	grams	10	100
400 m²	grams	10	100

Mixed Measuring Units

With large volumes of vegetative material associated with trees and large shrubs, it is more practical to estimate weights in pounds rather than grams. The conversion factor on a *per plot* basis, when weights are collected in pounds for a 96 ft² plot, is 454. Likewise, vegetative material associated with grasses, forbs, and small shrubs is more easily estimated in grams. Therefore, on a per plot basis, weights collected in grams for a .1 acre plot would convert to 2.2 pounds per acre (conversion for a 0.01 acre plot is 0.22).

Adjustment Factors

The ideal situation for determining production data for each individual species is to sample them when they are at their maximum production. With a diversity of species, it is impossible to make these determinations at one point in time during the growing season. Therefore, the production of each species must be reconstructed to reflect total annual production. This is accomplished using the conversion factors described previously.

Green Weight Adjustment Factor

This is the procedure for converting green weight, which is the weight of vegetation estimated or collected in the field, to air-dry weight.

ADW percentages for various types of plants at different stages of growth are provided in Appendix 7. These percentages are based on currently available data and are intended for interim use. As additional data from field evaluations become available, these figures will be revised. ADW percentages listed in Appendix 7 can be used for other species having growth characteristics similar to those of the species listed.

States that have prepared their own tables of air-dry percentages on the basis of actual field experience can substitute them for the tables in Appendix 7. Be sure to check with the local office of the NRCS for their latest ADW percentage tables. It is recommended that local field offices develop these tables for local conditions and species. Some interpolation must be done in the field to determine air-dry percentages for growth stages other than those listed. If ADW percentage figures have not been previously determined and included in ADW percentage tables, or if ADW conversion factors need to be checked, retain and dry enough harvested material samples to determine ADW percentages.

The relationship of green weight to ADW varies according to such factors as exposure, amount of shading, time since last rain, and unseasonable dry periods. Several samples of plant material should be harvested and air-dried each season to verify the factors shown in Appendix 7 or to establish factors for local use.

Double Sampling Adjustment Factor

This is the adjustment factor calculated from the double sampling process (see Double Sampling—Estimating and Havesting, number 6). The harvested weights are divided by the estimated weights. A factor of more than 1.0 indicates the estimate is too low. A factor lower than 1.0 indicates the estimate is too high.

Air-dry Weight Adjustment Factor

This is the appropriate ADW percent in decimals from tables and charts that convert green weight to ADW based upon various stages of growth.

Utilization Adjustment Factor

This is the percent of the plant's current growth remaining at the time of sampling. Biomass lost as a result of herbivory (e.g., livestock, wildlife, insects) must be recognized and re-created in order to provide a more accurate estimate of the total current year's annual production for individual species and the plant community. The utilization adjustment attempts to restore this missing amount of production. The examiner determines the percent of the current year's growth that remains. This is actually the reverse of percent utilized. For example, if utilization on a plant species averages 30 percent on the production transect, the percentage of the plants remaining would be 70 percent. Thus, the adjustment entered for that particular species would be 0.70. Utilization may vary throughout the weight estimate plots, requiring an estimate of the average use to determine the adjustment.

Growth Adjustment Factor

This is the percent of growth (in decimal form) that has occurred up to the time plot data is collected. The values entered can reflect the growth curves for the site (as listed in some site descriptions), or it could be based upon locally developed growth curve data for each species.

Reconstructing the Present Plant Community

The existing plant community at the time of inventory must be reconstructed to the normal annual air-dry production before it can be compared with the reference plant community. The reconstruction must consider physical, physiological, and climatological factors that affect the amount of biomass measured (i.e., weighed or estimated) for a species at a specific point in time. The present plant community is reconstructed by multiplying the measured weight of each species by a reconstruction factor. The reconstruction factor formula is:

$$\text{Reconstructed} = \frac{(GW)\ (A)\ (B)\ (C)}{(D)\ (E)}$$

where:

GW = Green weight
 A = Plot size conversion factor
 B = Double sampling adjustment factor, if appropriate
 C = Percent of air-dry weight (ADW)
 D = Percent of plant biomass of each species that has not been removed
 E = Percent of growth of each species that has occurred for the current growing season

Ocular Estimation of Production Data

Ocular estimates of production for an entire site, as opposed to estimating production on individual plots, is the quickest and easiest technique. However, with inexperienced people, the reduced accuracy resulting from this technique limits the use of the data. Ocular estimates are useful in quickly determining the similarity index of a site (see Chapter 5) for use in mapping plant communities and in stratifying SWAs for sampling purposes.

The following procedure is used in to become proficient at estimating production for an SWA.

1. Estimate production, in pounds per acre or kilograms per hectare, of individual species on the site.

2. Estimate production of individual species on a series of random plots.

3. Compute production in pounds per acre or kilograms per hectare from the random plots. To further check these estimates, harvest or double sample according to procedures addressed in the double sampling section of this document.

4. Repeat procedure until proficiency is attained.

Although this procedure misses some species of minor importance, it provides a useful check on estimates.

Inventory Level of Intensity

The minimum standard for an ecological site inventory is production by species. The level or intensity at which the production of a plant community is determined depends on the intended use of the data. Ocular estimates are the quickest and easiest technique for determining production, but may result in reduced accuracy, limiting use of the data. Estimating production of individual species on production plots is more time consuming, but the accuracy of the data is significantly increased, especially if plots are periodically harvested and weight-unit weights are adjusted accordingly. Harvesting is the most accurate technique, but because of the additional time required for collection is seldom used except in research-type efforts. A combination of harvesting and estimating or double sampling is probably the best technique for documenting the production on the site. Double sampling is the technique NRCS uses for documenting new ecological site descriptions and revising existing descriptions. Even with the estimating technique, frequent clipping studies (harvesting) should be conducted to calibrate the observer's eye.

Production Data for Documenting Rangeland Ecological Sites

Data to be used for preparing rangeland ecological site descriptions and grouping soils into rangeland ecological sites are to be obtained by the double-sampling procedure. All documented production and composition data are to be recorded on the Vegetation Production Worksheet in Appendix 4. Specific procedures for documenting an ecological site description can be found in the NRSC National Range and Pasture Handbook, Chapter 4.

Chapter 5 - Similarity Index

Definition and Purpose of a Similarity Index

THE PRESENT PLANT COMMUNITY on an ecological site can be compared to a reference community by the calculation of a similarity index. In most cases, the reference community is the historic climax plant community or potential natural community.

A similarity index is a comparison of the present state of vegetation on an ecological site in relation to the kinds, proportions, and amounts of vegetation with other vegetation communities the site is capable of producing. It is expressed as the percentage of a plant community that is presently on the site. To make the comparison, the reference vegetation communities must be described in sufficient detail in the ecological site description. As ecological site descriptions are revised and further developed, they should also include descriptions of other common vegetation communities that can exist on the site.

The similarity index can provide managers with a starting point for establishing specific management objectives. It also provides a means of determining the successional status (Table 8).

Table 8 - Successional Status

Similarity Index	Successional Status
0-25%	early
26-50%	mid
51-76%	late
77-100%	(potential natural community)

Determining Similarity Index

A similarity index determines how closely the current plant community resembles either the potential natural community or some other reference community. In order to make this determination, the existing plant community must be inventoried by recording weight, in pounds per acre, for each species present. In determining the similarity index, the allowable production of a species in the existing plant community cannot exceed the production of the species in the reference plant community. If plant groups are used, the present reconstructed production of a group cannot exceed the production of the group in the reference plant community.

Table 9 demonstrates how the similarity index is determined on four different reference communities for a loamy upland 12-16 PZ ecological site. (Refer to Chapter 3 for information on Ecological Sites and Appendix 3 for the ecological site description.) Table 9 shows only one plant from each plant group described in the ecological site description. This is for illustrative purposes to show the calculation of the similarity index. In actual practice, it is desirable to list all species found on the sample transect. This example assumes the current plant community has been reconstructed to actual annual production.

On the similarity index form in Table 9, each species is listed in column B, along with the production for the reference plant community in column C (pounds per acre). Current annual production for each species is shown in column D. The allowable production in column E is determined by using the smaller of the two production amounts (columns B or C). The total allowable production represents the amount of the reference plant community that is currently present on the site. The similarity index is determined by dividing the total allowable production (total of column E) by the total production for the reference community (total of column C).

Table 9 - Examples of Similarity Index Determinations on a Loamy Upland 12-16 PZ Ecological Site

Determination of similarity index to the potential natural community

Management Unit or Allotment: *Rockin' Raindrop*   Examiner: *Someone's name*

Ecological Site: *Loamy Upland 12-16 PZ*   Location: *Center of Horse Pasture*

Reference Plant Community: *Native midgrass (HCPC)*   Date: *8/30/96*

A	B	C	D	E
Plant Group	Species Name	Production/acres in reference plant community (from ecological site description)	Annual production in lb/acre (actual or reconstructed)	Pounds Allowable
1	Sideouts grama and others from Group 1	400-500	25	25
2	Bluegrama and others from Group 2	150-250	25	25
3	Threeawn species others from Group 3	50-100	40	40
4	Bush muhley and others from Group 4	50-100	25	25
5	Curly mesquite and others from Group 5	10-50	20	20
6	Fall witchgrass and others from Group 6	10-50	30	30
7	Six week threeawn and others from Group 7	10-50	15	15
8	Wild daisy and others from Group 8	100-150	5	5
9	Tansy mustard and others from Group 9	10-15	5	5
10	Range ratany and others from Group 10	50-100	50	50
11	Jumping cholla and others from Group 11	10-50	160	30
12	Mesquite and others from Group 12	10-20	600	20
Totals	Average Year	1000	1,000	290

Similarity Index to Native Midgrass Community = 29% (Total of E divided by total of C)

Table 9 - (continued)

Determination of similarity index to the mesquite-short grass vegetation state on loamy upland 12-16 PZ site

Management Unit or Allotment: *Rockin' Raindrop* Examiner: Someone's name
Ecological Site: *Loamy Upland 12-16 PZ* Location: *Center of Horse Pasture*
Reference Plant Community: *Mesquite-Short Grass* Date: *8/30/96*

A	B	C	D	E
Plant Group	Species Name	Production/acres in reference plant community (from ecological site description)	Annual production in lb/acre (actual or reconstructed)	Pounds Allowable
1	Sideouts grama and others from Group 1	15-50	25	25
2	Bluegrama and others from Group 2	300-400	25	25
3	Threeawn species and others from Group 3	10-50	40	40
4	Bush muhley and others from Group 4	0	25	0
5	Curly mesquite and others from Group 5	15-100	20	20
6	Fall witchgrass and others from Group 6	0	30	0
7	Six week threeawn and others from Group 7	0	15	0
8	Wild daisy and others from Group 8	10-50	5	5
9	Tansy mustard and others from Group 9	0	5	0
10	Range ratany and others from Group 10	10-50	50	50
11	Jumping cholla and others from Group 11	0	160	0
12	Mesquite and others from Group 12	15-100	600	100
TOTALS		665	1,000	265

Similarity Index to Mesquite-Short Grass Community = 40% (Total of E divided by total of C)

Table 9 - (continued)

Determination of similarity index to the native-short grass vegetation state on loamy upland 12-16 PZ site

Management Unit or Allotment: _Rockin' Raindrop_   Examiner: _Someone's name_
Ecological Site: _Loamy Upland 12-16 PZ_   Location: _Center of Horse Pasture_
Reference Plant Community: _Native-Short Grass_   Date: _8/30/96_

A	B	C	D	E
Plant Group	Species Name	Production/acres in reference plant community (from ecological site description)	Annual production in lb/acre (actual or reconstructed)	Pounds Allowable
1	Sideouts grama and others from Group 1	15-50	25	25
2	Bluegrama and others from Group 2	300-400	25	25
3	Threeawn species and others from Group 3	15-50	40	40
4	Bush muhley and others from Group 4	0	25	0
5	Curly mesquite and others from Group 5	15-150	20	20
6	Fall witchgrass and others from Group 6	0	30	0
7	Six week threeawn and others from Group 7	0	15	0
8	Wild daisy and others from Group 8	15-50	5	5
9	Tansy mustard and others from Group 9	0	5	0
10	Range ratany and others from Group 10	15-50	50	50
11	Jumping cholla and others from Group 11	trace	160	0
12	Mesquite and others from Group 12	trace	600	0
TOTALS		630	1,000	165

Similarity Index to Native-Short Grass Community = 26% (Total of E divided by total of C)

Table 9 - (continued)

Determination of similarity index to dense mesquite vegetation state on loamy upland 12-16 PZ site

Management Unit or Allotment: _Rockin' Raindrop_ Examiner: _Someone's name_
Ecological Site: _Loamy Upland 12-16 PZ_ Location: _Center of Horse Pasture_
Reference Plant Community: _Dense Mesquite_ Date: _8/30/96_

A	B	C	D	E
Plant Group	Species Name	Production/acres in reference plant community (from ecological site description)	Annual production in lb/acre (actual or reconstructed)	Pounds Allowable
1	Sideouts grama and others from Group 1	0	25	0
2	Bluegrama and others from Group 2	0	25	0
3	Threeawn species and others from Group 3	15-50	40	40
4	Bush muhley and others from Group 4	15-50	25	25
5	Curly mesquite and others from Group 5	0	20	0
6	Fall witchgrass and others from Group 6	0	30	0
7	Six week threeawn and others from Group 7	0	15	0
8	Wild daisy and others from Group 8	0	5	0
9	Tansy mustard and others from Group 9	0	5	0
10	Range ratany and others from Group 10	0	50	0
11	Jumping cholla and others from Group 11	0	160	0
12	Mesquite and others from Group 12	500-600	600	555
TOTALS		620	1,000	620

Similarity Index to Native-Short Grass Community = 100% (Total of E divided by total of C)

(Table adapted from the NRCS National Range and Pasture Handbook, 1997)

Many older ecological site descriptions document the extent of individual species within the historic climax plant community by percent of composition rather than pounds per acre. Production figures are presented as total weights (pounds per acre) for normal years, favorable years, and unfavorable years.

To calculate a similarity index, species composition must be converted to pounds per acre. Because the percent of composition for each species is based on total air-dry weight (ADW), conversion of the percentages to pounds per acre is easy. Simply multiply the percentage for each species by the total pounds per acre for an average year to arrive at the number of pounds per acre for each species. Table 10 converts the percent composition (column 2) from the reference community (found in an ecological site description) to pounds per acre (column 3). Also shown is the annual production (column 4) and the allowable production (column 5). Column 5 is determined by the smaller of the two amounts (column 3 or 4).

Table 10 - Reference Community

Reference Community				
Symbol	% of PNC (Reference Community)	Average Year 1000 lbs/acre	Annual Production	Allowable Production
Grasses	75-85	750/850	180	180
Group 1	40/50	400-500	25	25
Group 2	15-25	150-250	25	25
Group 3	5-10	50-100	40	40
Group 4	1-5	10-50	25	25
Group 5	1-5	10-50	20	20
Group 6	1-5	10-50	30	30
Group 7	1-5	10-50	15	15
Forbs	5-10	50-100	10	10
Group 8	10-15	100-150	5	5
Group 9	1-5	10-50	5	5
Shrubs/Trees	5-10	50-100	810	100
Group 10	5-10	50-100	50	50
Group 11	1-5	10-50	160	30
Group 12	1-2	10-20	600	20

In determining allowable production, it is important not to exceed the production of the reference community relative to each species, plant group, or life form. In Table 10, the annual production of plant groups 1 through 10 does not exceed production in the reference community. In addition, the total annual production of grasses and forbs does not exceed production in the reference community.

In plant groups 11 and 12, annual production is much higher than allowed in the reference community. Therefore, the most production that can be credited is 50 and 20 pounds per acre respectively (high end of column 3). It is also important not to exceed the allowable production for all shrubs and trees (groups 10, 11, and 12). However, the total annual production for all shrubs and trees is 810 pounds and the allowable production is 100 pounds. Since plant group 10 has already been credited with the 50 pounds allowable, the remaining plant groups (11 and 12) can total no more than 50 pounds. Group 12 is given credit for 20 pounds, leaving 30 pounds for group 11.

Determining Similarity Index to the Potential Natural Community

When compared to the potential natural community, the similarity index represents the percent of the potential natural community present on the site. This provides a basis for describing the extent and direction of change that has occurred. The similarity index, coupled with the state and transition model, can help predict changes that could occur.

Determining Similarity Index to Other Vegetation States or Desired Plant Community

Determining the similarity index of the existing plant community to one or more of the possible vegetation states in the site description may be desirable. After management objectives have been developed, one specific plant community may be identified as the desired plant community. Once the desired plant community has been identified, it is appropriate to determine the similarity index of the existing community to the desired plant community.

Procedures for determining a similarity index for other vegetation communities are the same as described for the historic climax plant community. Table 9 shows similarity index determinations for some of the other vegetation states described in the loamy upland 12-16 PZ. These determinations use the same transect data used in Table 9. Refer to Chapter 3 for information on ecological sites and Appendix 3 for the ecological site description. These examples show only one species from each plant group.

Chapter 6 - Field Procedures

Minimum Standards

THE MINIMUM STANDARDS REQUIRED for an ecological site inventory are production and composition by air-dry weight (ADW) by species. The number of plots selected depends on the purpose for which the estimates are to be used, uniformity of the vegetation, and other factors. A minimum of 10 plots should be selected for collecting production data used in documenting rangeland ecological sites or for other interpretive purposes. If vegetation distribution is very irregular and 10 plots will not give an adequate sampling, additional plots can be selected. If the inventory design dictates it, fewer than 10 plots can be used.

Sampling Precision

Most uses of ecological site inventory data would not require the calculation of a sample size necessary to achieve a given level of precision at a given confidence level. Quantitative monitoring studies would be one situation requiring this calculation. However, if an inventory plan calls for a specified level of precision, refer to Sample Size Equation number 1, pages 346–350 of *Measuring and Monitoring Plant Populations*, BLM Technical Reference 1730-1. To use this equation (or the software program discussed in the next paragraph), an estimate of the standard deviation is needed. This can be obtained by taking an initial sample of quadrats and calculating the standard deviation of the set of total production values obtained from this

sample. The standard deviation of a set of values is easily calculated using the statistics mode or function on a hand calculator configured with that option or by using the standard deviation formula (also called "worksheet function") on a computer spreadsheet (e.g., the appropriate formula in Microsoft Excel is STDEV).

The easiest way to calculate the sample size for an ecological site inventory is to use the freeware program, PC SIZE: Consultant, which runs on any DOS or Windows machine. Instructions on obtaining and using it are given at the Web site associated with the book, *Monitoring Plant and Animal Populations: A Handbook for Field Biologists* by C. L. Elzinga, D. W. Salzer, J. W. Willoughby, and J. P. Gibbs, Blackwell Science Inc., 2001, at

http://www.esf.edu/course/jpgibbs/monitor/popmonroot.html

Once there, click on "Chapter 9, Statistics," then on "Instructions for Using DTSTPLAN and PC-SIZE: Consultant to Estimate Sample Size and Conduct Post Hoc Power Analyses." You'll then get a PDF file that tells how to download PC SIZE: Consultant and how to use it.

Site Write-up Area

For sampling and planning purposes, the landscape is divided into map units called site write-up areas (SWAs). A SWA is defined as the smallest geographical unit delineation to be used as a base for collecting vegetation data and resource information. It is the smallest mapped soil- vegetation unit. SWA delineations are the culmination of mapping ecological sites, vegetation communities, and administrative boundaries. Each individual SWA should consist of only one ecological site and one plant community. The only exception would be if two or more soil- vegetation complexes are so intermingled that individual ecological sites cannot be delineated. SWAs may be mapped down to a minimum of 6 acres. Within a single soil-vegetation unit (ecological site and plant community), for management purposes, SWA boundaries can be set on administrative boundaries such as allotments, pastures, wildlife habitat areas, or watersheds. The exact criteria for subdividing on administrative boundary lines must be documented in the inventory plan.

In order to compile data on a management unit or grazing allotment basis, SWAs must not cross accurately located management unit or allotment boundaries. SWAs may also be delineated on soil mapping unit or pasture boundaries as specified in the inventory plan. The more detailed the mapping, the greater the options are for interpretation of the data. A unique SWA number is assigned to each SWA delineated. The number consists of one alpha character and a consecutive 3 digit number (e.g., A001, F139, S091).

Field Inventory Mapping

Mapping must be done by trained vegetation specialists, wildlife biologists, foresters, soil scientists, and hydrologists (for riparian areas)

working closely together. Field mapping consists of delineating SWAs based on present plant communities (e.g., ecological sites, forestland ecological sites, or forest types). Field mapping should be completed prior to resource data collection. If the inventory plan identifies the need to stratify SWAs for vegetation data collection, the entire inventory area must be mapped first. It is desirable to complete mapping a year in advance of collecting vegetation data.

Mapping Process With a Completed Soil Survey

In areas where soil survey and ecological site descriptions are complete, an ecological site-soil series correlation should be available in the final soil survey report. The survey report may also identify soil series that support forestland ecological sites or forest types (habitat types) where the potential plant communities have already been defined.

Where Order II soil surveys are completed and ecological site interpretations have been made, boundaries of ecological sites can generally be determined directly from the soil map.

Order III mapping describes individual soil and plant components at association or complex levels. Mapping unit descriptions have been developed that describe each association component and include locations on the landscape and percentages of each soil. Individual ecological sites must be delineated if individual soils in the association have different potential historic climax plant communities.

Mapping Process Without a Completed Soil Survey

In areas where soil surveys are not completed, the NRCS must be contacted to obtain any available soil or ecological site data. The NRCS may be able to assist in training and in establishing the mapping legend. The mapping team must work together in the field to achieve consistency in SWA delineation based upon ecological sites, forestland ecological sites, or forest types. The soil scientist must ensure that soils are considered in delineations. If at all possible, a soil survey should be completed prior to or concurrently with delineation of ecological sites.

Mapping Ecological Sites

The first step in mapping SWAs is the mapping of ecological sites. Based on soils information and field reconnaissance, ecological sites are delineated on aerial photos.

Present Vegetation

Ecological sites are subdivided based on changes in plant communities. Significant changes in the following factors must be considered in delineating present vegetation communities:

1. Vegetation species composition (kinds, proportions, and amounts of present vegetation)
2. Vegetation ground cover
3. Vegetation height
4. Vegetation age class (especially in forested areas)
5. Topography
6. Other factors identified in the inventory plan

To assist in this effort, current vegetation communities can be mapped as standard vegetation subtypes. Vegetation types are designated according to vegetation aspect. A complete listing is given in Appendix 8. Table 11 lists some of the more common types.

Table 11 - Common Standard Vegetation Subtypes

Type	Subtype	Code
Grass	Short Grass	1001
	Mid Grass	1002
	Tall Grass	1003
Grasslike	Sedge	2001
	Rush	2002
Perennial Forbs	Perennial Forbs	3001
Shrub	Black Greasewood	4001
	Creosote Bush	4011
	Winterfat	4015
	Mesquite	4021
	Saltbush	4030
	Mixed Desert Shrub	4037
	Sagebrush	4040
	Mtn. Mahogany	4056
	Bitterbrush	4057
	Mountain Shrub	4060
	Snakeweed	4071
	Broadleaf Trees	5000
	Conifers	6000
	Pinyon	6097
	Juniper	6098
Broadleaf Trees	Willow	5074
Conifer	Douglas Fir	6001
Cryptogams		7000
Barren		8000
Annual Grass		9000
Other		9999

Successional Status Classification

If appropriate, ecological sites should be further subdivided based on the successional status of the existing plant community. This is usually apparent on the ground as a change in the plant community. Each distinct soil-vegetation unit should be placed in a successional status class by making visual estimates of species production (see ocular estimation of production data in Chapter 4). The mapping team should complete the Similarity Index Form (Appendix 9) to record these initial successional status determinations. To make this initial determination of succession status, compare the present plant community with that of the potential natural community. For the existing plant community, count as allowable production no more than the maximum weight shown on the ecological site description for any species in the climax community. Total the allowable production of all potential natural community species to indicate the relative similarity index. The rating must be between 0 and 100, depending on how closely the existing plant community resembles the potential natural community for the ecological site. These estimated similarity indices can be useful in a stratification effort.

Forest Types

Forest types are divided into stands—uniform plant communities of trees as to timber type, age class, vigor, height, ground cover, and stocking. The smallest delineated unit within a forest type is the SWA or stand. The mapping team must assign a SWA number to each delineated SWA.

Feature Mapping

Any permanent cultural, topographic, and biological features, as well as existing improvements, such as fences, roads, or water developments not shown on existing maps should be indicated on aerial photographs. Barriers to livestock, wildlife, or wild horse and burros should be noted.

Water Resources

Show all water resources, such as marshes, reservoirs, springs, seeps, or streams.

Photo Scale

The recommended standard photo scale for an ecological site inventory is 1:24,000. The minimum size delineation for SWAs is about 6 acres for distinct wildlife habitat areas, such as riparian areas for food and cover and cliffs or promontories for raptors. Table 12 shows minimum size delineations.

Table 12 - Photo Scale Minimum Size Delineations

Scale	Acres	Inches/Miles
1:20,000	4.0	3.16
1:24,000	6.0	2.64
1:31,680	10.0	2.0

Stratification

Stratification is grouping together similar SWAs for sampling purposes. To be stratified, a SWA must be composed of similar soil-vegetation units. Since production data from one SWA will be used for other SWAs in the stratum, it is extremely important that sites within the stratum be virtually identical. If there is a doubt whether they are the same, keep them separate.

The size of the geographical area to be stratified is determined and documented in the inventory plan. The complexity of the ecological situation, as well as local needs, determines whether stratification is made by allotment, group of allotments, environmental impact statement (EIS) area, planning unit, or field office. The inventory plan sets forth the criteria for stratification including the

number of SWAs that need to be sampled. The following protocols are recommended (Table 13).

Table 13 - Recommended Protocols for Stratification

SWAs in Stratum	Number of SWAs Transected
1 - 3	1
4 - 6	2
7 - 10	3

All strata are assigned a number and listed. The SWAs within a stratum should also be listed (Table 14).

Table 14 - Stratum Listing and SWA Listing by Stratum

Stratum Listing						
Stratum Listing						
Stratum Number	SWA Number	Ecological Site Number	Vegetation Subtype	Ecological Condition	Percent Slope	Slope Aspect
0001	B001	034XY001U	1002	M	10	N
0002	B002	034XY002U	4041	E	10	N
SWA Listing by Stratum						
Stratum Number	SWA Number	Ecological Site Number	Vegetation Subtype	Ecological Condition	Percent Slope	Slope Aspect
0001	B001	034XY001U	1002	M	10	N
0001	B013	034XY001U	1002	M	10	N
0001	B021	034XY001U	1002	M	10	N
0001	B023	034XY001U	1002	M	10	N
0001	B033	034XY001U	1002	M	10	N
0001	B043	034XY001U	1002	M	10	N
0001	B051	034XY001U	1002	M	10	N
0001	B063	034XY001U	1002	M	10	N
0002	B002	034XY002U	4041	E	10	N
0002	B006	034XY002U	4041	E	10	N
0002	B012	034XY002U	4041	E	10	N
0002	B018	034XY002U	4041	E	10	N
0002	B032	034XY002U	4041	E	10	N
0002	B041	034XY002U	4041	E	10	N

Stratums With One Transect

Data collected in the sampled transect applies to all the SWAs not sampled.

Stratums With Multiple Transects

To determine production data for each individual species, sum production totals for each sampled SWA and divide by the number of SWAs. For example, Black Grama (*Bouteloua Eriopoda*) occurs in sampled SWAs A001 and A005 at 3 and 7 pounds per acre respectively. SWA A009 was not sampled, but is in the same stratum. Total production for Black Grama for SWA A009 and all other unsampled SWAs in the same stratum would be 5 pounds per acre (3 lb/ac + 7 lb/ac = 10 lb/ac / 2 = 5 lb/ac). Species occurring in only one SWA would be treated the same way. Divide the total production by the number of SWAs sampled. For example, if Black Grama had not occurred in SWA A001, then production for Black Grama in unsampled SWAs would be 4 pounds per acre (7 lb/ac/ 2 = 3.5 or 4). Populate unsampled SWAs with the averaged production data.

Transect Locations

The mapping team must evaluate each SWA and recommend the most representative place to run the transect. Unless otherwise indicated by the mapping team, the following guidelines should be followed for locating the transect.

SWAs With One Soil-Vegetation Unit
(Figure 5)

Step 1. Determine the distance across the longest axis of the area to be sampled (SWA) in feet with a USGS 1:24,000 scale (orthophoto quads) map. Normally, a transect distance of 1/2 mile is adequate.

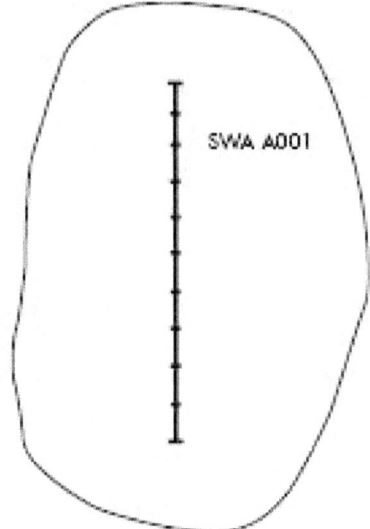

Figure 5 - One Soil-Vegetation Unit

Step 2. Divide the distance measured by 11 (the number of plots (10) plus one) so as not to sample on SWA boundary.

Step 3. Divide the distance between plots by the length of your pace (i.e., two steps) to get the number of paces between plots.

Step 4. Measure the compass bearing of the line by protracting off the orthophoto quad or aerial photo.

Step 5. Proceed to starting point.

Step 6. Take photograph(s) along the transect line.

Step 7. Pace the distance determined in Step 3 from the starting point to the first plot.

SWAs With Mixed or Mottled Patterns *(Figure 6)*

Where vegetation units are mixed or mottled, it will be necessary to randomly select plots in each soil-vegetation unit in order to collect a reliable sample. Soil-vegetation Unit A is one soil-vegetation unit that will be sampled by Transect 1. Soil-vegetation Unit B occurs as islands surrounded by Unit A. When collecting data for Transect 2, it will be necessary to divide Transect 2 into segments and locate some of the 10 plots on each island of Unit B. Both transects are within SWA F139.

The percentage of each soil-vegetation unit within the SWA is recorded on the Vegetation Production Worksheet in Appendix 4.

Other Options for Transect Layout *(Figures 7a and 7b)*

This option uses the same procedures used in the "SWAs With One Soil-Vegetation Unit" section, except the distance and compass bearing of each transect leg will have to be calculated.

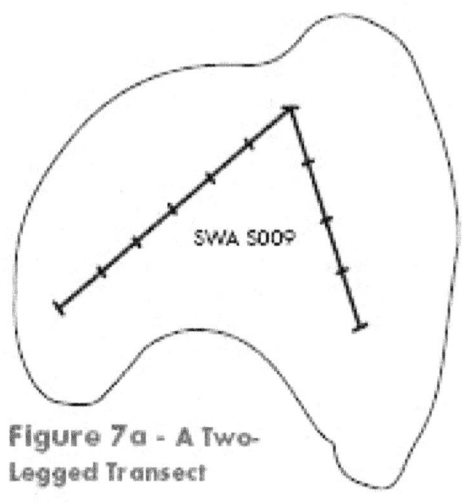

Figure 7a - A Two-Legged Transect

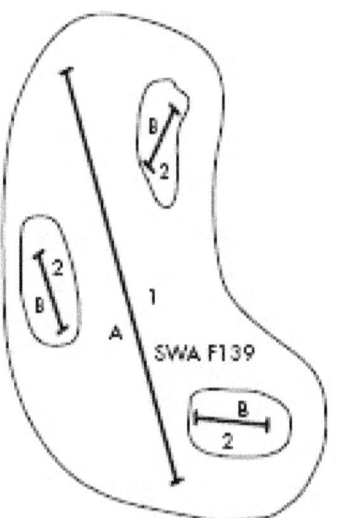

Figure 6 - Mixed or Mottled Soil-Vegetation Units

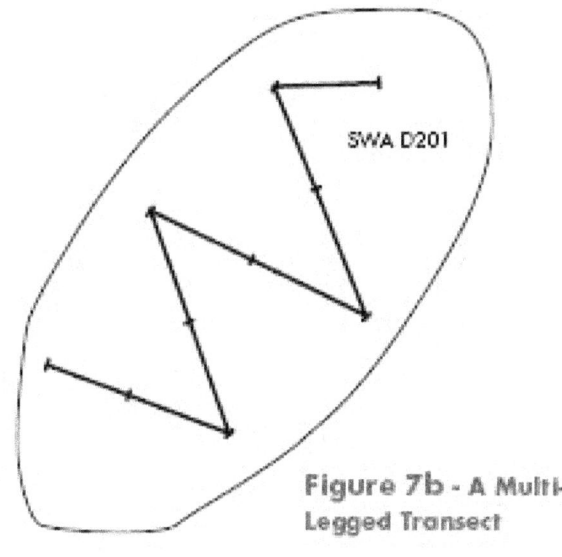

Figure 7b - A Multi-Legged Transect

Plot Sampling

Randomly select the beginning point of the transect. Determine the transect bearing and select a prominent distant landmark such as a peak or rocky point that can be used as the transect bearing point. Production plots are placed at the specified interval (i.e., paced or measured) along the transect bearing.

Vegetation Production Worksheet

The Vegetation Production Worksheet, with instructions, is located in Appendix 4. It is a sample form that can be used to record production data on the weight estimate plots. Field offices can use this form or develop forms to suit their needs. Remember, when using this form, to complete the top portion of the worksheet.

Several data elements (e.g., landform, soil texture class, and soil texture modifier) require specific codes. Some of these codes are identified in Appendix 10. Valid data entry values for other data elements on the form can be found in the Corporate Data Dictionary at:

http://sc2962.sc.blm.gov/datashopper/default.asp

Select **Applications** on the left side of the site. At the top of the site select **Elements**. At the inventory data systems site, a list of logical data elements will appear followed by a list of physical data elements. On the logical data element list, select **Detail** beside the name of the data element and the definition will appear. At the top, select **Valid Values**.

Chapter 7 - Data Storage

THE INVENTORY DATA (ID) SYSTEM, commonly referred to as IDS, is BLM's database for storing, querying, and analyzing soils, vegetation, and resource inventory data. This automated system includes vegetation data collected using the old Soil-Vegetation Inventory Method (SVIM) and the current ecological site inventory (ESI) method. It provides data for land use and allotment management planning. Data includes the physical characteristics of the site write-up area (SWA), such as slope, elevation, slope aspect, and landform; administration information, such as resource area, planning unit, allotment, recorder, and date of inventory; soils information, such as soil taxon name, soil survey number, and soil map unit number; ecological site information, such as site name and number and ecological status; vegetation data, such as species, estimated production, species composition, and life cycle and life form; and location information, such as section, township, range, acres, surface ownership, administrative agency, and jurisdictional agency.

The query process allows the user to determine, for instance, the number of acres in any particular ecological site, the occurrence of a particular species in a given allotment or ecological site, the total air-dry weight (ADW) production of a particular SWA or individual species, and the number of acres in a given successional status class. IDS can also be used to analyze the various plant communities that occur on a specific ecological site to select a desired plant community.

Ecological site inventory data should be input into IDS before field offices report the inventory complete. For information on entering data into IDS, contact the National Science and Technology Center (NSTC) in Denver Colorado.

Abbreviations and Acronyms

ADW	air-dry weight
BLM	Bureau of Land Management
CF	conversion factor
DOQQ	Digital Ortho Quarter Quads
DRG	Digital Raster Graphics
EIS	environmental impact statement
ESI	ecological site inventory
ESIS	Ecological Site Information System
FLPMA	Federal Land Policy and Management Act
FSSD	Field Soil Survey Database
GIS	geographic information system
GPS	global positioning system
IDS	Inventory Data System
IDSU	Inventory Data System Utilities
IHICS	Integrated Habitat Inventory and Classification System
MLRA	Major Land Resource Area
MLRU	Major Land Resource Unit
MOU	memorandum of understanding
NAPP	National Aerial Photography Program
NASIS	National Soil Information System (NRCS)
NBM	National Biology Manual
NCM	National Cartographic Manual
NEDC	National Employee Development Center (NRCS)
NFM	National Forestry Manual
NRCS	Natural Resources Conservation Service
NRPH	National Range and Pasture Handbook
NSH	National Soils Handbook
NSSH	National Soil Survey Handbook
NSTC	National Science and Technology Center (BLM)
NTC	National Training Center (BLM)
PNC	potential natural community
PRIA	Public Rangelands Improvement Act
PZ	precipitation zone
RISC	Range Inventory Standardization Committee
SSST	Special Status Species Tracking
STS	Species Tracking System
SVIM	soil-vegetation inventory method
SWA	site write-up area
USGS	United States Geographical Survey

Glossary

-A-

Age class: A descriptive term to indicate the relative age of plants.

Air-dry weight: The weight of vegetation after it has been allowed to dry to equilibrium with the atmosphere.

Allotment: an area of land designated and managed for grazing by livestock. Such an area may include intermingled private, State, or Federal lands used for grazing in conjunction with the public lands.

Annual production: The conversion of solar energy to chemical energy through the process of photosynthesis. It is represented by the total quantity of organic material produced within a given period of time.

Aspect: The visual first impression of vegetation or a landscape at a particular time or as seen from a specific point. The predominate direction of slope of the land. The seasonal changes in the appearance of vegetation.

At risk: Rangelands that have a reversible loss in productive capability and increased vulnerability to irreversible degradation based upon an evaluation of current conditions of the soils and ecological processes. At risk designation may point out the need for additional information to better quantify the functional status of an attribute.

Attribute (rangeland health): One of the three components that collectively define rangeland health; soil/site stability, hydrology function, and integrity of the biotic community.

-B-

Bare ground: All land surface not covered by vegetation, rock or litter.

Basal cover (area): The cross-sectional area of the stem or stems of a plant or all plants in a stand. Herbaceous and small woody plants are measured at or near ground level; larger woody plants are measured at breast or other designated height.

Biological soil crusts: Complex mosaics of any or all of the following: cyanobacteria, microfungi, algae, lichens, and mosses. They do not include club mosses (*Selaginella*) or tundra.

Biomass: The total amount of living plants and animals above and below ground in an area at a given time.

Boot stage: The growth stage when a grass seedhead is enclosed by the sheath of the uppermost (flag) leaf.

Brush: A term encompassing various species of shrubs or small trees usually considered undesirable for livestock or timber management. The same species may have value for browse, wildlife habitat, or watershed protection.

Bunch grass: A grass having the characteristic growth habit of forming a bunch; lacking stolens or rhizomes.

-C-

Canopy cover: The percentage of ground covered by a vertical projection of the outermost perimeter of the natural spread of foliage of plants. Small openings within the canopy are included. Canopy cover may exceed 100 percent and is synonymous with crown cover.

Climate: The average or prevailing weather conditions for a place over a period of years.

Composition: See species composition.

Cool season plants: Plants whose major growth occurs during the late fall, winter, and spring. Cool season species generally exhibit C3 photosynthetic pathways.

-D-

Desired plant community: Of the several plant communities that may occupy a site, it is the one that has been identified through a management plan to best meet the plan's objectives for the site. It must protect the site at a minimum.

Dominant species: Plant species or species groups, which by means of their number, coverage, or size, have considerable influence or control upon the conditions or existence of associated species.

-E-

Ecological process: Natural processes that function within a normal range of variation to produce and support specific plant and animal communities. Ecological processes include: water cycle (the capture storage and redistribution of precipitation); energy flow (conversion of sunlight to plant and animal matter); and nutrient cycle (the cycle of nutrients such as nitrogen and phosphorus through the physical and biotic components of the environment).

Ecological site: A kind of land with a specific potential natural community and specific physical site characteristics, differing from other kinds of land in their ability to produce distinctive kinds and amounts of vegetation and to respond to management. Ecological sites are defined and described with information about soil, species composition, and annual production.

Ecological site description: A written narrative of the description of soils, climate, vegetation, uses, and potential of a kind of land with specific physical characteristics to produce distinctive kinds and amounts of vegetation.

Ecological site inventory: A resource inventory that involves the use of soils information to map ecological sites and plant communities and the collection of natural resource and vegetation attributes. The sampling data from each of these soil-vegetation units, referred to as site write-up areas (SWAs), become the baseline data for natural resource management and planning.

Ecological status: See successional status.

Ecosystems: Organisms together with their abiotic environment forming an interacting system and inhabiting an identifiable space.

Energy flow: Conversion of sunlight to plant and animal matter; one of the ecological processes.

Erosion: Detachment and movement of soil or rock fragments by water, wind, ice, or gravity.

-F-

Facilitating practices: Practices that control or influence the management, movement, and handling of grazing animals. These practices include water developments (e.g., reservoirs, pipelines, wells, catchments), stock trails, fencing, salting, and herding.

Fauna: The animal species of a region.

Forb: Any herbaceous plant other than those in the Gramineae (true grasses), Cyperaceae (sedges), and Juncaceae (rushes) families (i.e., any nongrass-like plant) having little or no woody material on it; a broadleafed flowering plant whose above ground stem does not become woody and persistent.

Forestland: Land on which the potential natural community is dominated by trees.

-G-

Grass: Any plant of the family Gramineae (Poaceae).

Grasslike plant: A plant of the Cyperaceae (sedges) and Juncaceae (rushes) families, which vegetatively resembles a true grass of the Gramineae family.

Ground cover: The percentage of material, other than bare ground, covering the land surface. It may include live and standing dead vegetation, litter, cobble, gravel, stones, and bedrock. Ground cover plus bare ground would total 100 percent.

Growing season: That portion of the year when temperatures and moisture permit plant growth. In tropical climates, it is determined by the availability of moisture.

Gully: A furrow, channel, or miniature valley, usually with steep sides, through which water commonly flows during and immediately after rains or snow melt.

-H-

Half shrub: A plant with a woody base whose annually produced stems die each year.

Harvest: The removal of annual vegetation production from an area of land.

Herbaceous: Nonwoody plant growth.

Historic climax plant community: The plant community considered to best typify the potential plant community of an ecological site prior to the advent of European man.

-I-

Increaser: Those species that increase in amount for a given plant community, as a result of a specific abiotic/biotic influence or management practice.

Infiltration: The flow of a fluid into a substance through pores or small openings.

Invasion: The migration of organisms from one area to another area and their establishment in the latter.

Inventory: The systematic acquisition and analysis of information needed to describe, characterize, or quantify resources for land-use planning and management of the public lands.

-L-

Life form: Characteristic form or appearance of a species at maturity, such as a grass, forb, tree, or shrub.

Litter: The uppermost layer of organic debris on the soil surface; essentially the freshly fallen or slightly decomposed vegetal material.

-M-

Major land resource area: Broad geographic areas that are characterized by a particular pattern of soils, climate, water resources, vegetation, and land use. Each MLRA, in which rangeland and forestland occur, is further divided into ecological sites.

Management objective: A planned result to be achieved within a stated time period. Objectives are subordinate to goals, are specific with shorter timeframes, and have increased possibility of attainment. Time periods for completion and outputs or achievements are measurable and quantifiable.

Monitoring: The orderly collection, analysis, and interpretation of resource data to evaluate progress toward meeting objectives.

-N-

Native pasture: Land on which native vegetation (climax or natural potential plant community) is forest, but which is used and managed primarily for production of native plants for forage. Native pasture includes cutover forestland and forested areas that were cleared and used as cropland.

Native species: A species that is a part of the original fauna and flora of an area.

Nonvascular plants: Plants without specialized water or fluid conductive tissue (Xylem and phloem) that includes bryophytes, lichens and algae.

Noxious weed: An unwanted plant specified by Federal or State laws as being especially undesirable, troublesome, and difficult to control. It grows and spreads in places where it interferes with the growth and production of desired species.

Nutrient cycle: The cycle of nutrients, such as nitrogen and phosphorus, through the physical and biotic components of the environment; one of the ecological processes.

-O-

Objective: See management objective.

-P-

Pasture: A grazing area enclosed and separated from other areas by a fence or natural barrier.

Pedon: The smallest body of one kind of soil large enough to represent the nature and arrangement of horizons and variability in the other properties that are preserved in samples. Pedons extend down through all genetic horizons.

Perennial plant: A plant that has a life span of 3 or more years.

Phenology: The study of periodic biological phenomena that are recurrent (e.g., flowering, seeding), especially as related to climate.

Potential natural community (PNC): The biotic community that would become established if all successional sequences were completed without interference by man under the present environmental conditions. Natural disturbances are inherent in development. PNCs can include naturalized nonnative species.

-Q-

Qualitative: Observational type data that is recorded but not measured.

Quantitative: Collection of data by measuring vegetation or soil characteristics.

-R-

Rangeland: A type of land on which the indigenous vegetation (climax or natural potential) is predominantly grasses, grasslike plants, forbs, or shrubs and managed as a natural ecosystem. If plants are introduced, they are managed similarly. Rangeland includes natural grasslands, savannas, shrublands, many deserts, tundras, alpine communities, marshes, riparian zones, and wet meadows.

Rangeland health: The degree to which the integrity of the soil, vegetation, water, and air, as well as the ecological process of the rangeland ecosystem, are balanced and sustained.

Rangeland similarity index: The present state of vegetation and soil protection of an ecological site in relation to the potential natural community for the site.

Relict area: A remnant or fragment of the historic climax plant community that remains from a former period when it was more widely distributed.

Rill: A small intermittent water course with steep sides, usually only several centimeters deep. Rills generally are linear erosion features.

Riparian zone: The banks and adjacent areas of water bodies, water courses, seeps, and springs whose waters provide soil moisture sufficiently in excess of that otherwise available locally so as to provide a more moist habitat than that of contiguous flood plains and uplands.

Rock fragments: The unattached pieces of rock 2 mm in diameter or larger that are strongly cemented or more resistant to rupture. Rock fragments include all sizes that have a horizontal dimensions less than the size of a pedon. Rock fragments are described by size shape, and, for some, the kind of rock.

-S-

Sample: A set of sampling units as opposed to a single measurement.

Seral community: See seral stage.

Seral stage: The developmental stages of an ecological succession; synonymous with successional stage.

Shrub: A plant that has persistent woody stems and a relatively low growth habit, and that generally produces several basal shoots instead of a single bole. It differs from a tree by its low stature, less than 5 meters (16 feet), and nonarborescent form.

Slope aspect: The predominate direction of slope of the land.

Soil: The unconsolidated mineral and organic material on the immediate surface of the earth that serves as a natural medium for the growth of land plants. The unconsolidated mineral matter on the surface of the earth that has been subjected to and influenced by genetic and environmental factors of parent material, climate (including moisture and temperature effects), macro and microorganisms, and topography.

Soil association: A kind of map unit used in soil surveys comprised of delineations, each of which shows the size, shape, and location of a landscape unit composed of two or more kinds of component soils or component soils and miscellaneous areas, plus allowable inclusions. The individual bodies of component soils and miscellaneous areas are large enough to be delineated at the scale of 1:24,000. Several bodies of each kind of component soil or miscellaneous areas are apt to occur in each delineation, and they occur in a fairly repetitive and describable pattern.

Soil classification: The systematic arrangement of soil units into groups or categories on the basis of their characteristics. Broad groupings are made on the basis of general characteristics and subdivisions on the basis of more detailed differences in specific properties.

Soil inclusion: One or more polypedons or parts of polypedons within a delineation of a map unit, not identified by the map unit name (i.e., it is not one of the named component soils or named miscellaneous area components). Such soils or areas are either too small to be delineated separately without creating excessive map or legend detail, occur too erratically to be considered a component, or are not identified by practical mapping methods.

Soil map unit: A collection of soil areas or miscellaneous areas delineated in a soil survey. They may encompass one or more kinds of soil or one or more kinds of soil and miscellaneous areas, such as a rock outcrop. They are identified by a unique map symbol in a survey area. There are four kinds of map units: consociations, complexes, associations, and undifferentiated groups.

Soil survey: The systematic examination, description, classification, and mapping of soils in an area. Soil surveys are classified according to the kind and intensity of field examination.

Species composition: The proportions of various plant species in relation to the total on a given area. May be expressed in terms of relative cover, relative density, or relative weight.

State: A recognizable, resistant, and resilient complex of soil and vegetation.

Steady state: Vegetation states that are resistant to change. These plant communities change only as a result of a natural event that is beyond the normal range of events or normal human actions.

Stratification: the grouping together of similar site write-up areas (SWA) for sampling purposes. SWAs must have the same ecological site, forestland ecological site, or forest type in the same successional status class, or present vegetation community.

Structure (soil): The combination or arrangement of primary soil particles into secondary units or pedons. Secondary units are characterized on the basis of size, shape, and grade (degree of distinctness).

Structure (vegetation): The height and area occupied by different plants or life forms in a community.

Succession: The progressive replacement of plant communities on a site that leads to the potential natural plant community (i.e., attaining stability). Primary succession entails simultaneous succession of soil from parent material and vegetation. Secondary succession occurs following disturbances on sites that previously supported vegetation and entails plant succession on the more mature soils.

Successional status: The present state of vegetation and soil protection of an ecological site in relation to the potential natural community for the site. Successional status is the expression of the relative degree to which kinds, proportions, and amounts of plants in a community resemble that of the potential natural community. The four classes of successional status ratings, expressed in terms of similarity to the potential natural community, are: 0-25 percent early seral class, 26-50 percent mid seral, 51-76 percent late seral and 76-100 percent PNC.

Succulent: Juicy, watery or pulpy, as the succulent stems of cacti.

-T-

Threshold: The boundary between any and all states, or along irreversible transitions, such that one or more primary ecological processes has been irreversibly changed and must be actively restored before returning to a previous state is possible.

Transition: A shift in plant composition that results in relatively stable states, as reflected in composition and structure. These shifts can occur by natural forces or as a result of human actions.

Transition pathway: The mechanism that causes a change in plant community from one steady state to another (e. g., fire, drought, grazing, rest, chemical and mechanical treatment).

Tree: A woody perennial, usually single-stemmed plant, that has a definite crown shape and characteristically reaches a mature height of at least 5 meters (16 feet). Some plants, such as oaks (Quercus spp.), may grow as either trees or shrubs.

Trend: The direction of change in a vegetation attribute or successional status observed over time.

-V-

Vascular plant: Plants with vessels that conduct sap throughout the plant.

Vegetation: Plants in general, or the sum total of the plant life above and below ground in an area.

Vegetation attribute: The quantitative features or characteristics of vegetation that describe how many, how much, or what kind of plants are present. The most commonly used attributes are frequency, cover, density, production, structure, and composition.

Vegetation manipulation practices: Practices that are directed at changing vegetation production, species composition, and erosion control. These practices include root plowing, seeding, pitting, chaining, prescribed fire, herbicide application, prescribed grazing, and livestock exclusion.

Vegetation type: A kind of plant community with distinguishable characteristics described in terms of the present vegetation that dominates the aspect or physiognomy of the area.

-W-

Warm season plants: Plants whose major growth occurs during the spring, summer, or fall and that are usually dormant in winter.

Water cycle: The capture, storage, and redistribution of precipitation.

Watershed: The total area of land above a given point on a waterway that contributes runoff water to the flow at that point. A major subdivision of a drainage basin.

Weather: The current state of the atmosphere with regard to wind, temperature, cloudiness, moisture, and atmospheric pressure.

Woodland sites: See forestland.

Bibliography

Batson, F.T., P.E. Cuplin, and W.A. Crisco. 1987. Riparian area management: The use of aerial photography to inventory and monitor riparian areas. USDI, BLM/YA/PT-87/021+1737. Denver, Colorado. 16pp.

Despain, D.W., P.R. Ogden, and E.L. Smith. 1991. Comparative yield method for estimating range production. In: B. Ruyle, ed. Some Methods for Monitoring Rangelands and other Natural Area Vegetation. Extension Report 9043, University of Arizona, College of Agriculture, Tucson.

Elzinga, C.L., D.W. Salzer, and J.W. Willoughby. 1998. Measuring and monitoring plant populations, BLM Technical Reference 1730-1. BLM/RS/ST-98/005+1730. Bureau of Land Management, National Applied Resource Sciences Center. Denver, Colorado. 477 pp.

Gabriels, P. C. J. and J.V. Van Den Berg. 1993. Calibration of two techniques for estimating herbage mass. Grass and Forage Science (1993) Vol. 48:329-335.

Krebs, C.J. 1989. Ecological methodology. Harper & Row, New York, NY.

Pechanec, J.F. and G.D. Pickford. 1937. A weight-estimate method for the determination of range or pasture production. J. Amer. Soc. Agron. 29:894-904.

Smith, E.L. and D.W. Despain. 1991. Dry-weight rank method of estimating plants species composition. In: G.B. Ruyle, ed. Some methods for monitoring rangelands and other natural area vegetation. Extension Report 9043, University of Arizona, College of Agriculture, Tucson.

Stringham, T. K., W. C. Krueger, and P. L. Shaver. 2001. States, transitions, and thresholds: further refinement for rangeland applications. Agr. Exp. Sta. Oregon State University. Special Report 1024. 15 pp.

USDA, Natural Resources Conservation Service. 1997. Inventorying, classifying and correlating Juniper and Pinyon communities to soils in western United States. Grazing Lands Technology Institute. Fort Worth, Texas.

___. 1997. National Range and Pasture Handbook. Washington, DC.

___. 1996. National Soil Survey Handbook, 430-VI-NSSH. Washington, DC.

USDA, Soil Conservation Service. 1976. National Range Handbook. Washington, DC.

USDI, Bureau of Land Management. 1992. Procedures for ecological site inventory—with special reference to riparian-wetland areas. BLM Technical Reference 1737-7. BLM/SC/PT-92/004+1737. Denver, Colorado. 135 pp.

___. 1984. Manual Handbook 4410-1, National Range Handbook. Washington, DC.

Vermeire, L.T. and R.L. Gillen. 2001. Estimating herbage standing crop with visual obstruction in tall grass prairie. J. Range Managment, 54:57-60.

Wiegert, R.G. 1962. The selection of an optimum quadrat size for sampling the standing crop of grasses and forbs. Ecology 43:125-129.

Appendix 1 - Aerial Photography

BLM started flying aerial photography projects on a regular basis in the late 1960s. In general, where there are large blocks of BLM land ownership, there is usually resource scale aerial photo coverage.

Scale: Usually 1:24,000, some 1:12,000 (Northern California, Western Oregon), 1:15,840 or 1:31,680

Film Type: Mostly Natural Color or False Color Infrared (CIR), some Black and White

Years Flown: For a particular area, there may be only 1 year of coverage or multiple years/cycles of coverage.

The frequency of flights varies from State to State. Oregon has flown consistently from the 1950s through the present (Western Oregon in particular). Colorado, Idaho, New Mexico, Utah, and Wyoming typically have two cycles of coverage for most areas. Arizona, California, and Nevada typically have two cycles of coverage for only selected areas. Montana mostly has only one cycle of coverage (typically mid 1970s through the early 1980s only).

Special project photographs have also been completed on selected areas, typically for riparian or photogrammetric purposes.

Scale: Usually 1:2,400 to 1:6,000 range

Film Type: Mostly Natural Color or False Color Infrared(CIR).

Years Flown: Generally only 1 year of coverage. In some cases, there may be multiple years/cycles of coverage.

To determine what BLM coverage exists (e.g., geographic area, year flown, scale, film type) and obtain copies of the flight line indexes, contact the BLM State or field office aerial photo/remote sensing contact. Most of the original film is stored at BLM's aerial photo archive in Denver. To order photo reproductions or determine coverage, you can also contact the BLM's National Science and Technology Center (NSTC) in Denver. Contact Larry Cunningham (303-236-6382/ Fax 6564) or Connie Slusser (303-236-7991/Fax 7990) at:

NSTC, ST-122,
BLM, Bldg. 50, Denver Federal Center
PO Box 25047
Denver, Colorado 80225-0047

Other sources of aerial photo coverage include:

U.S. Geological Survey
Earth Science Information Center
Bldg. 810, Denver Federal Center
Denver, Colorado 80225
303-202-4200

They have an extensive listing of their own coverage, plus what other Federal, State, and county agencies, and private companies have.

U.S. Department of Agriculture
Aerial Photography Field Office
PO Box 30010
Salt Lake City, Utah 84130
801-975-3503

They have their own coverage (Forest Service land, Farm Service Agency, and NRCS (previously ASCS and SCS)).

There is also the National Aerial Photography Program (NAPP). This program was started in 1987, with 5-year cycles for reflights. Most States have been flown three times. This program covers the entire country and may be more recent than typical BLM coverage.

Scale: 1:40,000

Film Type: Black and White for most 1990 and newer and CIR for 1987-1989

Years Flown: 1987 to present (3 cycles)

For determining coverage and photo numbers for NAPP you can:

- Contact your BLM State Office or the BLM Denver office.
- Contact the USGS or USDA (see above).
- Go to the USGS Web site.

For placing aerial photo orders from the NAPP, contact the USGS or USDA.
For reproduction costs, please contact the BLM, USGS, or USDA for the film they have.
Note: BLM was a contributor from 1987 through 1994, thus we get a price break for these years.

Appendix 2 - Soil Map Unit Delineations

Draft
Technical Note
RIPARIAN-WETLAND
SOIL MAP UNIT DELINEATIONS

04/21/92
Prepared by George J. Staidl, NSRT

Background

Soil survey techniques and procedures guiding soil surveys, soil scientists, and SCS SSQA staff have generally concentrated on the major soil components and map unit delineations with substantial acreage. These procedures, in conjunction with cartographic policy, only allow for a closed line delineation or general spot symbols to identify unique areas. Use of delineations or spot symbols is highly dependent upon the scale of the photobase maps. Many unique areas are comprised of riparian zones and wetlands of minor acreage. These unique areas contain contrasting soils and are usually the most vegetatively productive soils within any survey area. The typical field mapping process identifies these areas with a broadly defined spot symbol or as contrasting soil inclusions within map units. This is a result of not identifying the riparian-wetland mapping objectives in the soil survey area MOU and the emphasis put upon the soil scientist to increase their production of acres mapped. The result is a tradeoff in detail of mapping and reduced ability to provide soil information concerning riparian and wetland areas.

The present farm bill and other congressional legislation have emphasized preservation and management of these unique riparian-wetland areas. They are, for the most part, the more productive and fragile parts of the ecosystem. The soil survey and cartographic procedures presently in use are not conducive to identifying and delineating many of these smaller areas as soil map units. These areas need to be part of a permanent soil database. Without this data, quality information cannot be disseminated to the user to meet the legislative needs. New techniques need to be explored, tested, and implemented within the soil survey process to give the soil scientist the tools to incorporate past, present, and future data into soil survey activities.

Statement of Needs

As noted previously, congressional legislation has pointed out a need for additional soil survey information applicable to riparian and wetland areas. Availability of this information for total resource planning and conservation practice application is also vitally important in the decision making process. It is recognized that data collection should be initiated in many areas thought to be of less importance, or at least unmappable, using the policy and techniques available to the soil scientist at the time.

Implementation would require that the resulting soil and plant data obtained be incorporated into a permanent database. This would maximize its utility for present and future data dissemination. This can be accomplished by developing a mechanism to identify these unique areas on field sheets, orthophoto quads, and in a GIS database where available. To maintain a permanent database, some modification of procedures will be needed. This should include modification of requirements using innovative cartographic techniques, map unit design, map unit descriptions, correlation to the series and phase level, and data entry to the soil survey database. Field applications would take into account only that which is normally expected for delineation and documentation common to other map units. Addressing the inequities of the present procedures will minimize the need for continued onsite investigation where soil and vegetation data is presently maintained in a nonpermanent form. Positive changes to the present system will maximize soil data availability for use by managers and others.

Requirements

A. Any modifications to the existing soil survey procedures will be applicable to a soil survey where:

1. GIS capability may or may not be available.

2. Targeted areas will include:

   a. New SSA(s)
   b. Ongoing SSA(s)
   c. Newly completed SSA(s)
   d. SSA(s) undergoing update

3. The need exists for information on unique lands (riparian-wetland areas and others) and is presently unavailable.

B. Development and expansion of procedures for implementation will:

1. Be incorporated into any existing GIS database where the potential exists.

2. Allow for the correlation of minimal acreage unique soils to the series level. This will initiate data entry into the soil survey database.

3. Allow for the correlation of minimal acreage unique soil mapping units. This will initiate data entry into the soil survey database.

4. Provide techniques for unique delineations and spot symbols that will represent map units, but do not meet the present cartographic requirements.

5. Provide procedures to use the unique delineations and spot symbol map units to represent spatial area and allow for acreage determination.

6. Allow for the description of spatial area concepts for the unique delineation and spot symbol map units as a component in map unit descriptions.

C. Proposed methods for use in soil survey areas:

1. Line segment (e.g., dot to dot or line break to line break) vector format.

   a. Determine and designate the representative delineations line segment width for each map unit (e.g., the map unit line segment represents an average width of 120 feet). This information, along with the line length and scale of map, will determine map unit acreage.

b. Suggested line width groupings are 1-50, 50-100, 100-150, and 150-200 feet. Areas that are greater than 200 feet wide will typically be located by an enclosed line polygon.

c. Assign a map unit symbol to each line segment using a leader technique. A unique Alpha or Numeric code, representing an average width within a line segment group, will be assigned as the last character in the map unit symbol. An example of a symbol is 103X, where "103" is the map unit name and "X" indicates an average width of 75 feet in the 50-100 feet group.

d. Utilize the existing drainage spot symbols as line segment breaks to minimize map clutter.

2. Spot symbols.

a. Use ad hoc symbols or a dot to represent a map unit.

b. Determine the acreage that each spot symbol or dot represents for the map unit (e.g., averages 2.5 acres). Suggested spot symbol grouping are <1, 1-2, 2-3, 3-4, and 4-5 acres. Those areas that are greater than 5 acres will typically be located by an enclosed line polygon.

c. Assign a map unit symbol to each spot symbol or dot using the leader technique. A unique Alpha or Numeric code representing an average acreage for the spot symbol group will be assigned as the last character in the map unit symbol. An example of a symbol is 103P, where "103" is the map unit name and

"P" indicates an average acreage of .5 acres for the <1 acre group.

D. Field procedures for soil survey areas:

1. Field check the area to be mapped in terms of the normal map unit concept.

2. Design a map unit using accepted soil survey procedures.

3. Determine if the map unit is a consociation, association, complex, or undifferentiated group.

4. Identify each major and minor component soil within the proposed map unit, preferably at the soil series level, and assign phases as needed.

5. Obtain all necessary documentation for soils, vegetation, hydrology, etc.

6. Using the documentation collected, correlate each major soil component of the map unit to the series level.

7. Assign each new map unit its own unique map unit symbol and display with representative line segments or spot symbols on the soil map.

8. Designate the representative line segment width and spot symbol acreage in each applicable map unit description.

9. Determine acreage for each line segment or spot symbol on each completed soil map.

10. Continue using accepted National Cooperative Soil Survey procedures throughout the survey.

E. Delineation and map symbol application will be as follows:

1. Line segments or spot symbols will be on original field sheets and orthophotoquad soil maps.

2. Line segments or spot symbols will be on registered mylar overlays with a stable base map.

3. Line segments or spot symbols will be transferred to scribe coat of orthophotoquad for publication processes.

4. Line segments and spot symbols will be digitized as part of the GIS database.

F. Data permanence procedure within the soil survey area:

1. Identify and implement the soil mapping options noted in (E) above that are applicable to the soil survey area status.

2. Undergo the review and final correlation process common in any soil survey as outlined in the National Soils Handbook.

3. Prepare and process all necessary soil series and map unit information into the National Soil Survey Database for future access of output data.

Appendix 3 - Ecological Site Description

United States Department of Agriculture, Natural Resources Conservation Service

Ecological Site Description
Rangeland
Site name: Loamy Upland 12-16 PZ
Site number: R - 041XC313AZ
Major land resource area: 41 - Southeastern Arizona Basin and Range
Interstate correlation: None

Physiographic features
This site occurs on fan and stream terraces. The elevations range from 3,200 to 5,200 feet above sea level. This site occurs on all aspects of the slope. The slopes on this site range from 1% to 15%.

Climatic features
Frost-free period: 170-220 days - Feb.20 - Nov.25
Freeze-free period: 180-225 days - Feb.15- Nov.30
Mean annual precipitation: 12-17 inches
Mean annual air temperature: 68.0 °F
Mean annual soil temperature: 70.0 °F

Monthly moisture and temperature distribution:

	Mean precipitation (in)	Percent precipitation (%)	Mean temperature (°F)
January	0.93	6.65	51.1
February	0.78	5.6	53.8
March	0.71	5.2	57.8
April	0.45	3.2	65.0
May	0.21	1.5	73.2
June	0.29	2.1	82.9
July	2.82	20.3	86.2
August	2.56	18.4	84.0
September	2.07	14.9	80.4
October	1.15	8.3	70.4
November	0.87	6.3	58.7
December	1.05	7.6	52.0
Mean annual	13.89	100	68.0

Other climatic features
Precipitation in the subresource area ranges from 12 to 16 inches yearly in the eastern part with elevations from 3,600 to 5,000 feet. Precipitation in the western part ranges from 13 to 17 inches yearly with elevations from 3,300 to 4,500 feet. Winter - summer rainfall ratios are 40:60 in the west side of the resource area to 30:70 in the eastern portion of the area. Summer rains fall July - September, originate in the Gulf of Mexico and are convective, usually brief, intense thunder-storms. Cool season moisture tends to be frontal,

originates in the pacific and Gulf of California, and falls in widespread storms with long duration and low intensity. Snow rarely lasts more than 1 day. May and June are the driest months of the year. Humidity is generally very low.

Temperatures are mild. Freezing temperatures are common at night from December through April, however, temperatures during the day are frequently above 50 °F. Occasionally in December to February, brief periods of 0 °F temperatures may be experienced some nights. During June and rarely during July and August some days may exceed 100 °F. Frost free days range from 170 to 220.

The cool season plants start growing in the early spring and mature in early summer. The warm season plants take advantage of the summer rains and are growing and nutritious from July through August. Warm season grasses may remain green throughout the year.

Associated water features

Nonstream characteristics: None
Stream characteristics: None

Soils

The soils on this site are very deep. They have been formed in loamy alluvium of mixed origin. Surfaces range from very gravelly sandy loam to loam. Sandy loam surfaces can be no thicker than 4 inches (8 inches for gravels). These soils all have argillic horizons near the surface. Plant-soil moisture relationships are good. Soil surfaces are dark colored.

Major Soil Taxonomic Units correlated to this site include:
> Whitehouse 1, sl
> Bernardino 1(15% slope)
> Caralampi 1, sl (15% slope)
> Sasabe 1, sl
> Enzian 1, sl
> Forrest 1
> McAllister 1

Plant communities

Historic climax plant community: The interpretive plant community for this site is the Historic climax plant community. This community is dominated by warm-season perennial grasses. All the major perennial grass species on the site are well dispersed throughout the plant community. Perennial forbs and a few species of low shrubs are well represented on the site. The aspect of this site is that of an open grassland.

Major plant species composition

This list of plants and their relative proportions are based on near normal years. Fluctuations in species composition and relative production may change from year to year dependent upon abnormal precipitation or other climatic factors. The historic climax plant community has been determined by study of rangeland relict areas, or areas protected from excessive grazing. Trends in plant communities going from heavily grazed areas to lightly grazed areas, seasonal use pastures and historical accounts have also been used.

Grasses and Grasslikes 750-850 pounds per acre

Scientific plant symbol	Common name	Group	Pounds per acre	Percent by weight	Percent allowable for group
BOCU	sideoats grama	1	400-500		40-50
ERIN	plains lovegrass	1			
BOBA3	cane beardgrass	1			
BOER4	black grama	2	150-250		15-25
BOGR2	blue grama	2			
BOHI2	hairy grama	2			
BOCH	sprucetop grama	2			
LYPH	wolftail	2			
ARIST	threeawn species	3	50-100	5-10	5-10
DICA8	Arizona cottontop	4			5-10
SEMA5	plains bristlegrass	4			
HECO10	tanglehead	4			
TRSE	crinkleawn	4			
MURI	purple muhly	4			
MUPO2	bush muhly	4			
HIBE	curly mesquite	5	10-50		1-5
BORO2	rothrock grama	5			
BOFI	slender grama	5			
SPCR	sand dropseed	5			
MUE	aparejograss	5			
PAOB	vine mesquite	6	10-50		1-5
LECO	fall witchgrass	6			
PAHA	Hall panicum	6			
TRPU2	fluffgrass	6			
PAMU3	pima pappusgrass	6			
SPCO4	spike dropseed	6			
LEDU	green sprangletop	6			
ENDE	spike pappusgrass	6			
SIHY	bottlebrush squirreltail	6			
TRMU	slim tridens	6			
BORA	purple grama	6			
BOTR2	red grama	6			
ARAD	six weeks threeawn	7	10-50		1-5
AROL	annual threeawn	7			
BOBA2	six weeks grama	7			
BOAR	needle grama	7			
VUOC	six weeks fescue	7			
PAAR	Arizona panicum	7			
BRLAR4	Arizona brome	7			
LEFI	red sprangletop	7			
EUN2	Mexican sprangletop	7			
ERAR	desert lovegrass	7			
ERDI	spreading lovegrass	7			
CHVI	featherfinger grass	7			

Forbs 100 to 150 pounds per acre

Scientific plant symbol	Common name	Group	Pounds per acre	Percent by weight	Percent allowable for group
SIPR2	sida	8	100-150		10-15
TAAU	talinum	8			
ERDI4	wild daisy	8			
SPNA4	desert globemallow	8			
BRDE	small matweed	8			
HODE	hog potato	8			
BRPU2	covena	8			
ANTU	wind flower	8			
HASP2	spiny haplopappus	8			
CRCO11	leatherweed	8			
OEPR	evening primrose	8			
VIAM	vetch	8			
FRAR2	snake cotton	8			
PLIN	trailing four o'clock	8			
STPA4	wire lettuce	8			
POGR5	yerba de venado	8			
DYPO	dogbane dyssodia	8			
BAAB	bahia	8			
TILA2	honeymat	8			
ASTRA	loco species	8			
LOSAB	mares fat	8			
PORTU	pursley species	8			
ASTER	annual aster	8			
TRADE	spiderwort	8			
CINE	thistle	8			
PLIN3	Indianwheat	8			
ERTE13	bull filaree	8			
PEPA2	chinch weed	8			
ERIOG	annual buckwheat	8			
ANODA	anoda	8			
ARABI	rock cress	8			
DYAC	Texas dyssodia	8			
BAMU	desert marigold	8			
JAGR	slender janusia	8			
PSORA	breadroot	9	10-15		1-5
VIAN	annual goldeneye	9			
DEPI	tansy mustard	9			
PHYSA	tomatillo	9			
GALLI	blanket flower	9			
CHENO	lambsquarter	9			
AMTE3	fiddleneck	9			
LUSP2	desert lupine	9			
PHLOX	phlox	9			
LILE	blue flax	9			
BELY	green eyes	9			
PENA	desert holly	9			
ERDI2	diffuse eriastrum	9			

Shrubs and Trees 100- 150 pounds per acre

Scientific plant symbol	Common name	Group	Pounds per acre	Percent by weight	Percent allowable for group
CAER	false mesquite	10	50-100		5-10
ERWR	shrubby buckwheat	10			
KRPA	range ratany	10			
ZIPU	desert zinnia	10			
ZIGR	Texas zinnia	10			
KRLA	spreading ratany	10			
OPAR2	pencil cholla	11	10-50		1-5
OPFU	jumping cholla	11			
OPEN	Engelmann pricklypear	11			
ECHIN3	hedgehog cactus	11			
MOMI	pincushion cactus	11			
CORYP	coryphantha	11			
OPVE	staghorn cholla	11			
OPLE	Christmas cholla	11			
ECWI	fishhook barrel cactus	11			
FOSP2	ocotillo	11			
AGPA	desert agave	11			
YUEL	soaptree yucca	12	10-20		1-2
YUBA	datil yucca	12			
EFTR	longleaf Morman tea	12			
LYCIU	wolfberry	12			
ATCA2	fourwing saltbush	12			
BAFT	yerba de pasmo	12			
PRJU	mesquite	12			
PAFL6	blue paloverde	12			
ACGR	catclaw acacia	12			
ACCO2	whitethorn	12			
MIBI8	catclaw mimosa	12			
MESC	twinberry	12			
JUMO	oneseed juniper	12			
NOMI	sacahuista	12			
PAAC3	retama	12			
HATE	burroweed	12			
GUSA2	broom snakeweed	12			
GUMI	threadleaf snakeweed	12			
MIDY	velvet-pod mimosa	12			
ELCE	tarbush	12			
PAMI5	littleleaf paloverde	12			
PSCO2	whitestem paperflower	12			
ZIOB	greythorn	12			

Ground cover and structure

	Height above the ground									
	Not applicable		6 - 12 inches		12 - 24 inches		24 - 60 inches		180 - 240 inches	
	% ground cover	% canopy cover	% ground cover	% canopy cover	% ground cover	% canopy cover	% ground cover	% canopy cover	% ground cover	%canopy cover
Trees									<1	1-3
Shrubs							2-3	5-7		
Forbs			2-3	5-7						
Grasses					10-12	20-25				
Litter	7-10									
Cryptogams	<1									
Coarse fragments	5-10									
Bare ground	60-70									

Total annual production

The historic climax plant community will produce approximately the following amounts of air dry vegetation per acre:

Favorable year: 1,500 lb/ac
Normal year: 1,000 lb/ac
Unfavorable year: 650 lb/ac

Ecological dynamics and major plant community types

With continuous heavy grazing, palatable perennial grasses, such as blue grama, hairy grama, sprucetop grama, sideoats grama, and plains lovegrass, decrease. Increasers under such circumstances include curly mesquite, threeawn species, and in places, false mesquite. With severe deterioration, shrubby species increase to the point of dominance. Mesquite forms the overstory with snakeweed and lesser amounts of burroweed in the understory. Cholla and pricklypear can also increase on the site. When present on the site, mesquite tends to be short, due to the presence of clay horizons at shallow depths in the soils.

Loss of porous surface soil causes a reduction in the sites ability to effectively use intense summer rainfall. Natural fire may have been important in the development of the historic climax plant community. Lehmann lovegrass can invade this site, but usually does not become dominant. The potential for the site to maintain its annual production is reduced by increasing mesquite canopy. Stable areas of the site can produce effective herbaceous covers with up to 10%–15% canopy cover of mesquite. In areas where half-shrubs dominate the understory, the potential production of perennial grasses is about 10% greater than the present production of halfshrubs once they are removed from the plant community by fire or other brush management.

There have been no special emphasis species identified on this site. As that information becomes available it will be included. Following is a description of the present day plant communities that can occupy this site. The diagram illustrates the transition pathways between the common plant communities on the site.

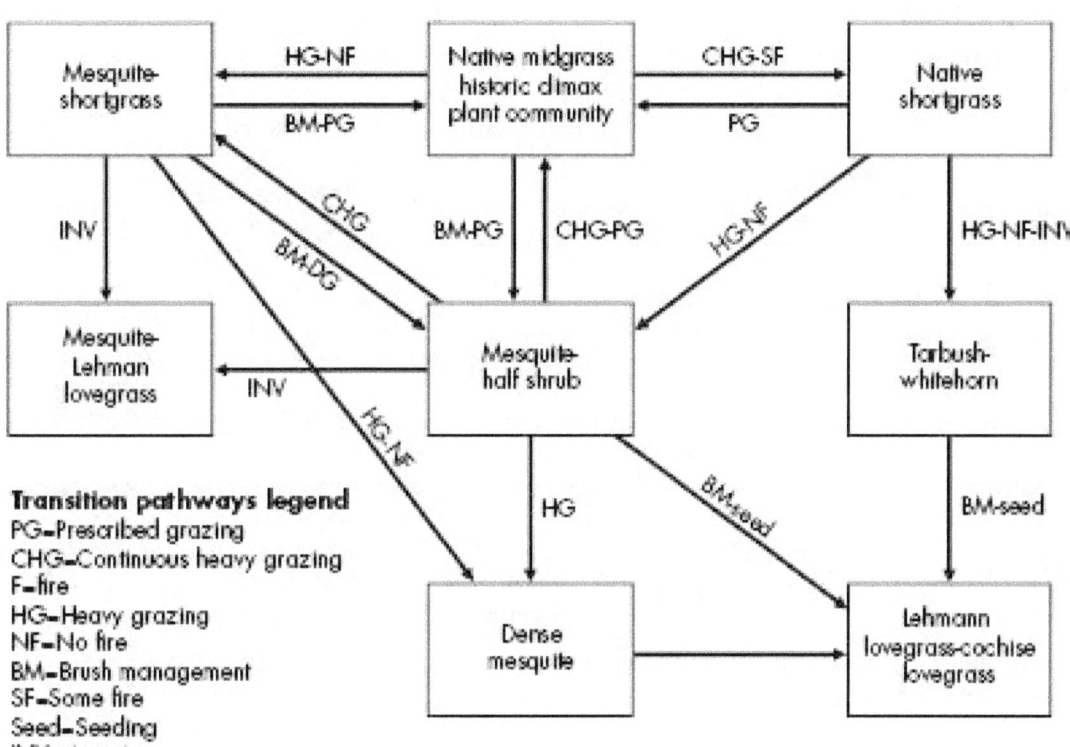

Transition pathways legend
PG—Prescribed grazing
CHG—Continuous heavy grazing
F—fire
HG—Heavy grazing
NF—No fire
BM—Brush management
SF—Some fire
Seed—Seeding
INV—invasion

Native midgrass-This is the historic climax plant community for this site. This plant community evolved through the holocene in the absences of grazing by large herbivores and with fire frequency of every 10 to 20 years. It exists all across the upper end of this MLRA especially on moderate slopes with very gravelly surfaces. The typical plant community description for this vegetation state is described in detail above.

Native short grass-This plant community exists all across the upper end of the MLRA. It is especially common on nearly level slopes with little or no gravel cover. It is characterized by a continuous cover of short grama grasses (blue, black, sprucetop), curly mesquite and low shrubs

(calliandra and krameria). It is stable unless basal cover falls below 5%–6% on 2%–3% slopes. Average production is less than historic climax plant community as the more shallow rooted community cannot fully exploit the soil, water, and nutrients available in average or better growing seasons. It is excellent for livestock grazing, but lacks mid-grass cover needed by some wildlife species (antelope fawns). The grass cover is easily thinned by drought, but usually recovers rapidly. The transition pathway included heavy grazing with some occurrence of fire. The water cycle has been severely altered, as has the nutrient cycle. This community occurs in the healthy, at risk and unhealthy recoverable categories.

The following represents the typical plant community of the vegetation state described as **Native-Short Grass**. Refer to the Historic climax plant community for the plants in each plant group.

Plant group	Pounds per acre
1	15-50
2	300-400
3	15-50
5	15-150
8	15-50
10	15-50
11	T
12	T

Total annual production 630 lb/ac (normal year)

Mesquite short grass-This plant community exists all across the MLRA. Mesquite canopy ranges from 1%–10%. The understory is a continuous cover of short grama grasses and/or curly mesquite. It is stable unless basal cover falls below 5%–6% on 2%–3% slopes. Production is always less than the historic climax plant community. Mesquite exploits the soil, water, and nutrients earlier in the spring and to a greater depth than the shallow rooted warm-season grasses. The grass cover is easily thinned by drought and may be slow to recover due to the presence of mesquite. It is good for livestock grazing, but the tree cover can interfere with livestock handling operations. The presence of mesquite allows species, such as mule deer and javelina, to use this site, but detract from its value as antelope habitat. The transition pathway includes heavy grazing, no fires, and a proximity to mesquite in bottom-lands. The ecological processes of water cycle, nutrient cycle, and energy flow have been severely altered. The hydrologic functioning of this site has been altered. This site occurs most often as at risk and unhealthy recoverable categories.

The following represents the typical plant community of the vegetation state described as **Mesquite-Short Grass**. Refer to the Historic climax plant community for the plants in each plant group.

Plant group	Pounds per acre
1	15-50
2	300-400
3	15-50
5	15-100
8	15-50
10	15-50
12	15-150

Total annual production 665 lb/ac (normal year)

Mesquite halfshrub/cacti-This plant community exists all across the lower and mid portion of the MLRA. Mesquite canopy ranges from 1%–10%. The understory is a diverse mixture of cacti, burroweed, broom snakeweed, and other shrubs. Perennial grasses exist in trace amounts only. The plant community is poor for livestock grazing, poor for some wildlife species (e.g. pronghorn antelope and scaled quail) and good for other wildlife species (e.g., mule deer, javelina, and gambel quail). Transition pathway is from mesquite short grass with continued heavy grazing and the absence of fire. Almost all the ecological processes on this site have been severely altered, and the site has lost some of the recovery mechanisms. In general, the site is not stable in this plant community and occurs most often as unhealthy recoverable category.

The following represents the typical plant community of the vegetation state described as

Mesquite-Shrub-Cacti. Refer to the Historic climax plant community for the plants in each plant group.

Plant group	Pounds per acre
2	15-50
3	15-100
4	15-50
7	15-50
11	15-150
12	500-600

Total annual production 750 lb/ac (normal year)

Dense mesquite-This plant community occurs all across the MLRA in small areas, especially historic heavy use areas, such as old homesteads, in horse pastures, along streams with perennial flow and other old watering locations, and also on archaeological sites. Mesquite canopy ranges from 10%–30%. The understory consists of scattered low shrubs, remnant perennial grasses, and annual species. This plant community is very poor for livestock grazing and poor quality habitat for most wildlife species. However, under the present hunting pressure in southern Arizona, the oldest and largest mule deer bucks use these mesquite thickets as hiding and escape cover. The site in this plant community is not stable. Often times so much of the soil surface has been lost under this condition that the site will not respond to treatment and the site potential has been lost. In some cases the erosion has so damaged the site that even the existing mesquite trees have difficulty surviving. Transition pathway is from mesquite short grass

with excessive grazing and no fires. This site occurs most as unhealthy recoverable and unhealthy unrecoverable categories.

The following represents the typical plant community of the vegetation state described as **Dense Mesquite**. Refer to the Historic climax plant community for the plants in each plant group.

Plant group	Pounds per acre
3	15-50
4	15-50
12	500-600

Total annual production 620 lb/ac (normal year)

Tarbush/Whitethorn-This plant community occurs throughout the eastern portion of the MLRA in areas where loamy upland is adjacent to limy sites that naturally support tarbush and whitethorn. Canopy cover of the two shrubby species usually exceeds 10%. The understory consists of scattered low shrubs, remnant perennial grasses and annuals. This plant community is very poor for livestock grazing and poor quality habitat for most wildlife species. The site under this plant community is not stable. Often so much surface soil has been lost that the site will not respond to treatment and the site potential has been lost. Transition pathway is from native mid-grass with heavy grazing, no fires, and a proximity to tarbush/whitethorn on adjacent limy sites. This site occurs most as unhealthy recoverable and unhealthy unrecoverable categories.

The following represents the typical plant community of the vegetation state described as **Tarbush-Whitethorn**. Refer to the Historic climax plant community for the plants in each plant group.

Plant group	Pounds per acre
1	15-50
2	15-50
3	15-100
4	15-100
8	15-50
10	15-50
12	500-600

Total annual production 800 lb/ac (normal year)

Mesquite-Lehmann lovegrass-This plant community occurs throughout the MLRA. In nearly all cases it has developed from mesquite native grasslands in the last 30 years. Livestock grazing, fire, and drought have all been demonstrated to enhance this invasion of loamy upland site wherever there is a seed source of Lehmann lovegrass. This plant community offers a great deal of stability to the site. Mesquite canopy is usually less than 10%. Lehmann production equals or exceeds native grass production. Species diversity is usually greatly reduced on this site once Lehmann lovegrass has become dominant. Under mesquite native grass conditions it is common to find 40 to 50 perennial plant species on this site. Under Lehmann dominance that figure will be 20 to 30 species. This plant community is good for livestock grazing. It is fair for some species of wildlife (mule deer and gambel quail). It is good for small herbivores (rabbits and mice) and generally poor for many other species, such as pronghorn antelope and scaled quail. Transition pathway is from mesquite short grass with heavy grazing, some

fires, and a Lehmann lovegrass seed source. The ecological processes on this site have been altered somewhat, and this site occurs as healthy, at risk, and unhealthy recoverable categories.

The following represents the typical plant community of the vegetation state described as **Mesquite-Lovegrass**. Refer to the Historic climax plant community for the plants in each plant group.

Plant group	Pounds per acre
2	15-50
8	15-50
10	15-50
12	50-150
13	1,200-1,400 (consists of introduced lovegrasses, such as Lehmann, Cochise, Boer, and Wilman)

Total annual production 1,425 lb/ac (normal year)

Lehmann lovegrass and/or Cochise lovegrass-This plant community occurs throughout the MLRA. It exists where mechanical brush management was used to control mesquite, tarbush, whitethorn, and cacti, and where lovegrass species were seeded. This plant community offers a great deal of stability to the site. Because of the nature of the grass species and the mechanical roughening of the soil surface, these communities generally produce 20–50% more than native grass communities. Although plant species diversity is low in these lovegrass communities, it is usually better than in the woody dominated plant community it replaced. This community is good to very good for livestock grazing, fair for some wildlife species pronghorn antelope and scaled quail), good for other species (rabbits and mice), and poor for such species as mule deer and javalina. The transition pathway is from either mesquite halfshrub/cacti or dense mesquite, with the inclusion of mechanical brush management and seeding of one or both of the lovegrass species. The ecological processes are functioning relatively similar to that of the historic climax plant community. This site most often occurs in the healthy category.

The following represents the typical plant community of the vegetation state described as **Lehmann lovegrass-Cochise lovegrass**. Refer to the Historic climax plant community for the plants in each plant group.

Plant group	Pounds per acre
1	15-50
2	15-100
8	15-50
10	15-100
13	1,250-1,450 (consists of introduced lovegrasses, such as Lehmann, Cochise, Boer, and Wilman)

Total annual production 1,495 lb/ac (normal year)

Plant Growth Curves

Growth curve number: AZ0001
Growth curve name: Native 1
Growth curve description: Native plant community with high similarity index and average growing conditions.

Jan.	Feb.	March	April	May	June	July	Aug.	Sept.	Oct.	Nov.	Dec.
5	5	5	3	2	2	20	20	18	10	5	5

Growth curve number: AZ0002
Growth curve name: Native 2
Growth curve description: Native plant community with low similarity index dominated by mesquite and cacti, and average growing conditions.

Jan.	Feb.	March	April	May	June	July	Aug.	Sept.	Oct.	Nov.	Dec.
5	5	5	10	15	25	10	5	5	5	5	5

Growth curve number: AZ0003
Growth curve name: Mesquite-Lehmann lovegrass
Growth curve description: Plant community dominated by mesquite with and understory of Lehmann lovegrass, average growing conditions.

Jan.	Feb.	March	April	May	June	July	Aug.	Sept.	Oct.	Nov.	Dec.
5	5	5	10	15	15	15	10	5	5	5	5

Animal community

The plant community on this site is well suited to grazing by both domestic livestock of all kinds and by wildlife at all seasons of the year. Currently the majority of the livestock use on this site is with mother cows in a cow-calf operation. Historic use has always been a cow/calf type operation, but there have been periods of large numbers of stocker cattle on these ranges. Sheep use has been slight historically. The main problem to the use and management of livestock on this site is the lack of natural water sources.

This site is important for many wildlife species. Major species include desert mule deer, pronghorn antelope, gambels quail, scaled quail, and black-tailed jackrabbit. Water developments are very important to these and other wildlife on this site. Being an open grassland, this site is also home to a variety of small herbivores, birds, and their associated predators. With the exception of pronghorn antelope, this site is mainly a forage area for larger wildlife species. The value of this site for food or cover requirements for specific wildlife species changes with the changes in the vegetation that occur from one plant community to another. Each plant community and each animal species must be considered individually. General information has been included here and in the ecological dynamic section of this site description.

Associated site-This site is associated with the Limy Upland 12-16 PZ and the Loamy Bottom sites.

Similar sites-With the historic climax plant community, this site is not similar enough to any other site to cause a problem or concern. As this site deteriorates it may easily be confused with other deteriorated sites, such as Limy Upland. Many sites will deteriorate into very similar plant communities.

Site Documentation

Author: Original WHN 1976
Revised DGR 1987

Supporting data for site development-The historic climax plant community has been determined by study of rangeland relict areas or areas protected from excessive grazing. Trends in plant communities going from heavily grazed areas to lightly grazed areas, seasonal use pastures, and historical accounts have also been used. The following transect and clipping data also documents this site. There are 21 permanent transect locations on this site.

Sampling technique	EC	GC	PC	PC
SCS-Range 417	10	15	15	3
SCS AZ-Range-1	1	7	10	13

Type locality:

Pima Co	Buenos Aires NWR, Sec. 19, T21S, R8E
Cochise Co.	Oak Ranch, Sec.2, T18S, R28E
Cochise Co.	Ft. Huachuca, Sec.17, T21S, R19E unsurveyed
Santa Cruz Co.	Santa Fe Ranch, Sec. 13, T23S, R14E
Pinal Co.	Tom Mix Hwy ROW, Sec.2, T10S, R13E

Field offices:

Casa Grande	Chandler
Douglas	Phoenix
Safford	San Carlos
Sells	Tucson
Willcox	

Relationship to other established classifications-This site would most closely fit A.W. Kuckler's Potential Natural Vegetation as unit number 58 Grama - Tobosa - Shrubsteepe. It most closely fits the Society for Range Management's Rangeland Cover Types as unit number 505 Grama - Tobosa Shrub.

Plant species index-(This section provides a cross reference for common names, scientific names, and national symbol. It will be generated by ESIS, no input required here.)

Other references (list other references used in the description or correlation of this site.)

Site approval-This site has been reviewed and approved for use.

State Rangeland Management Specialist

Date

Ecological site interpretations

Grazing
The plant community on this site is suitable for grazing by all classes of livestock at any season. With thin, course textured surfaces, and over argillic horizons, these soils become less effective in catching summer rainfall if the grass cover is disturbed or depleted. With a good grass cover, the clayey subsoil releases moisture slowly to the plants over the summer season. Lehmann lovegrass can invade this site slowly, but seldom forms a monotype. At the first sign of invasion, proper use of the native perennials must be practiced to avoid letting lovegrass spread. Herbaceous forage is deficient in protein in the winter. This site has no natural surface water associated with it; therefore, water development for livestock is necessary for utilization of this site.

Initial starting stocking rates will be determined with the landowner or decision maker. They will be based on past use histories and type and condition of the vegetation. Calculations used to determine an initial starting stocking rate will be based on forage preference ratings.

Forage preferences by season for cattle
(P = preferred, D = desirable, U = undesirable)

Plant species	Dec/Feb	March/May	June/Aug	Sept/Nov
Sideoats grama	U	P	P	P
Plains lovegrass	U	P	P	P
Cane beardgrass	U	D	P	D
Blue grama	D	P	P	P
Sprucetop grama	D	P	P	P
Curly mesquite	D	P	P	P
Hairy grama	D	P	P	P
Spidergrass	U	U	D	U
Red threeawn	U	D	U	U
Perennial forbs	P	P	P	P
False mesquite	U	P	D	P
Ratany species	P	P	D	P
Zinnia species	P	P	D	P
Mesquite	U (leaves)	P (new leaves)	P (beans)	P (beans)
Staghorn cholla (fruits)	P	D	P	P
Pricklypear (fruits)	U	U	P	P

Wildlife

This site has no natural surface water associated with it. Water developments are important to wildlife on this site. Being an open grassland, this site is home to a variety of small herbivores, birds, and their associated predators. Except for pronghorn antelope, this site is mainly a foraging area for the larger wildlife. There are no threatened or endangered wildlife species that rely on this site for any of their habitat requirements.

Guide to site plant use by selected wildlife species
(P = preferred, D = desirable, U = undesirable, X = used, but degree of utilization unknown)

Plant species	Desert mule deer	Pronghorn antelope	Gambels quail	Scaled quail	Blacktailed jackrabbit
Perennial grasses	2.5% diet	3% diet	P)seed	P)seed	P)foliage
Annual grasses	2.5% diet	3% diet	P)seed	P)seed	P)foliage
Annual forbs	P)green	P)green	P)sd/gr	P)sd/gr	P)foliage
Sida	P)foliage	P)foliage	P)seed		
Evolvulous	P)foliage	P)foliage			
Dychoriste	P)foliage	P)foliage			
Cudweed	P)foliage	P)foliage			P)foliage
Wild daisy	P)foliage	P)foliage	P)seed	X)seed	P)foliage
Globe mallow	P)foliage	P)foliage	P)seed	X)seed	P)foliage
Ragweed	D)foliage				P)foliage
Hog potato	X)foliage			P)seed	
Covena	P)foliage	X)foliage		X)seed	
False mesquite	P)lvs/twg	P)lvs/flw	P)seed	P)seed	X)foliage
Ratany species	P)lvs/twg				X)foliage
Zinnia	X)lvs/twg				X)foliage
Yerbe-de-pasmo	X)lvs/twg	X)leaves			
Mesquite	P)lvs/bn	P)bean	P)seed	P)seed	P)lvs/bn
Staghorn cholla	P)fruits	P)flw/frt	P)seed	P)seed	
Prickly pear	P)fruits	P)flw/frt	P)frt/sd	P)frt/sd	P)pads
Ocotillo	D)flowers	X)lvs/flw			
Barrel cactus	P)fruits	P)fruits	P)seed	P)seed	
Agave		P)flowers			

Hydrology data

The hydrology of this site is characterized by high intensity thunderstorms during summer months and, in winter, by low intensity frontal storms. From 60 to 70% of the annual moisture occurs during the summer months. The site has a porous soil surface that is resistant to erosion when perennial vegetation cover is sufficient to protect the site from damage. As basal cover is reduced, the surface soil is exposed to accelerated erosion and can be quickly lost. The clayey subsoil is more resistant to erosion, but is not able to sustain the original plant community. Deteriorated sites are characterized by low infiltration and excessive runoff. This site naturally delivers water to adjacent sites downstream by overland flow. Concentrated flow patterns are common and can easily become rills and gullies if cover is lost.

Wood products

Considerable amounts of mesquite occupy several present day plant communities. Wood products potential is low on this site. Mesquites remain small and shrubby because of the soils.

Appendix 4 - Vegetation Production Worksheet

Inventory Code _____ Management Unit or Allotment _____ Elevation _____ % slope _____ Slope Aspect _____ Landform _____

Site Write-up Area Number _____ Ecological Site Number _____ Ecological Site Name _____ Ecological Condition _____

Transect No. _____ % SWA _____ Soil Map Unit No. _____ Soil Taxon Name _____ Soil Phase Texture Class _____ Soil Phase Texture Modifier _____

Date _____ Recorder _____ Pasture Number _____ Estimate Total Production _____ (lb/ac) Vegetation Type _____

Stratum No. _____ Sampled? (circle)   Yes   No

Plant Species Symbol	Plant Species Common Name	Estimated Weight Units by Species (2)										Total Wt Units	Wt Unit Wt	Wt Meas gm/lb	Plot Size	Plot Size CF	Ade Adj	Unit Adj	Gwth Adj	Clp Plots Est Wt	Clp Plots Clp Wt	Clp/ Est CF	Total Weight LB/AC
	(Optional)	P-1	P-2	P-3	P-4	P-5	P-6	P-7	P-8	P-9	P-10												
(1)												(3)	(4)	(5)	(6)	(7)	(8)	(9)	(10)	(11)	(12)	(13)	(14)

Adjustments span columns (7)-(10). Double Sampling spans columns (11)-(13).

REMARKS:

Instructions for Filling out the Vegetation Production Worksheet

Be sure to complete the top portion of the worksheet. The following items deal with the vegetation portion of the transect.

Column 1   Enter the acceptable plant symbol from the USDA PLANTS Database at *http://plants.usda.gov/*. You can even download a list of species specific for your State. Entering the common name of the plant species is optional.

Column 2   For plots 1 through 10 (P-1 through P-10), enter an estimate of the number of weight units by species occurring in the appropriate plot(s), or the estimated weight by species occurring in the plots. The weight unit number can be expressed numerically (e.g. 6, 11.5). If weight by species is recorded, the number entered would be the total estimated weight for that species. For example, a number of 52 in P-3 would mean that 52 grams or pounds is the estimated weight for that species in plot 3.

Note: When double sampling is used to determine a correction factor, circle the plot numbers that are clipped.

Column 3   This column represents the summarized total number of weight units or weight by species occurring in plots 1 through 10 as estimated by the data collector.

Column 4   If weight units are entered in the plot data (2) columns, complete this column by entering the weight unit weight by species used by the data collector. If weight by species was entered in the plot data (2) columns, rather than weight units, enter 1 in this column.

Column 5   Enter the weight measure unit (grams or pounds) for the weight unit weight shown in column 4 or the summarized species weight listed in column 3.

Column 6   Enter the plot size used to estimate weight units or weight by species (e.g., plot sizes 9.6 ft2, 96 ft2, or .01 acre).

Column 7   Enter the plot size conversion factor (CF) from Tables 6 or 7 in Chapter 4.

Column 8   Enter the appropriate ADW percent in decimal form, from green weight conversions tables, Appendix 7 (Percent Air-Dry Weight Conversion Table), or local conversion tables.

Column 9   Complete this column only when the *current season's growth* of plant species has been removed by grazing. Enter the amount in decimal form (e.g., 0.25, 0.40, 0.60), which best reflects the percentage of the "*plant remaining*" after grazing utilization has occurred. For example, if a plant species averages 30 percent utilization in the production transect, the percentage of plant material remaining would be 70 percent. Thus, the adjustment entered for that particular species would be .70. Utilization may vary through the plots, requiring an estimate of the average use.

Column 10   Enter the cumulative percent of growth, in decimal form, that has occurred up to the time plot data is collected. The values entered can reflect the growth curves for the site (as listed in some site descriptions) or be based upon locally developed growth curve data for each species.

When doubling sampling is used to determine a correction factor, data will be recorded in columns 11 through 13; otherwise, these columns will be left blank.

Column 11   For each plant species occurring in the clipped plots, enter the total *estimated weight* (to nearest gram or pound) by multiplying the total weight units by the weight unit weight for all clipped plots.

Column 12   For each plant species occurring in the clipped plots, enter the *total clipped (harvested) weight* (to nearest gram or pound) for all clipped plots.

Column 13   To determine the correction factor, divide column (12) by column (11) for each species and enter to the nearest hundredth. A factor of 1 indicates the estimates are the same as the clipped weights. A factor below one 1 indicates estimates are high. A factor above 1 indicates estimates are low.

Total pounds per acre production result:

Column 14   This column represents the air-dry reconstructed weight in pounds per acre after considering all conversion, correction, and adjustment factors. Calculate pounds per acre (nearest pound) for each plant species by multiplying the number of weight units (3), times the weight of the individual weight unit (4), times the plot size conversion factor (7), times the ADW adjustment (8), times the clipped conversion factor (13). Divide by the utilization adjustment (9), times the growth adjustment (10). The formula is:

$$\text{Pounds per Acre} = \frac{\text{Columns (3) x (4) x (7) x (8) x (13)}}{\text{Columns (9) x (10)}}$$

Appendix 5 - Foliage Denseness Classes Utah Juniper

Guide for Determining Current Yield of Utah Juniper in Utah Upland Stony Loam (Juniper) Site

Crown diameter	Weight per tree	Current Yield Air Dry Pounds						
		10 trees	50 trees	100 trees	200 trees	300 trees	400 trees	500 trees
Sparse foliage								
1	0.1	1	5	10	20	30	40	50
2	0.3	3	15	30	60	90	120	150
3	0.6	6	30	60	120	180	240	300
4	1.0	10	50	100	200	300	400	500
5	1.3	13	65	130	260	390	520	650
6	1.6	16	80	160	320	480	640	800
7	1.9	19	95	190	380	570	760	950
8	2.3	23	115	230	460	690	920	1150
9	2.6	26	130	260	520	780	1040	1300
10	2.9	29	145	290	580	870	1160	1450
11	3.3	33	165	330	660	990	1320	1650
12	3.6	36	180	360	720	1080	1440	1800
13	4.0	40	200	400	800	1200	1600	2000
14	4.4	44	220	440	880	1320	1760	2200
15	4.7	47	235	470	940	1410	1880	2350
16	5.1	51	255	510	1020	1530	2040	2550
17	5.5	55	275	550	1100	1650	2200	
18	5.8	58	290	580	1160	1740	2320	
19	6.2	62	310	620	1240	1860	2480	
20	6.6	66	330	660	1320	1980	2640	
Medium foliage								
1	0.1	1	5	10	20	30	40	50
2	0.3	3	15	30	60	90	120	150
3	0.6	6	30	60	120	180	240	300
4	1.0	10	50	100	200	300	400	500
5	1.4	14	70	140	280	420	560	700
6	1.9	19	95	190	380	570	760	950
7	2.5	25	125	250	500	750	1000	1250
8	3.1	31	155	310	620	930	1240	1550
9	3.8	38	190	380	760	1140	1520	1900
10	4.6	46	230	460	920	1380	1840	2300
11	5.4	54	270	540	1080	1620	2160	2700
12	6.2	62	310	620	1240	1860	2480	
13	7.2	72	360	720	1440	2160		
14	8.1	81	405	810	1620	2430		
15	9.1	91	455	910	1820	2730		
16	10.2	102	510	1020	2040			
17	11.3	113	565	1130	2260			
18	12.4	124	620	1240	2480			
19	13.6	136	680	1360				
20	14.8	148	740	1480				

Guide for Determining Current Yield of Utah Juniper (continued)

Crown diameter	Weight per tree	Current Yield Air Dry Pounds						
		10 trees	50 trees	100 trees	200 trees	300 trees	400 trees	500 trees
Dense foliage								
1	0.1	1	5	10	20	30	40	50
2	0.3	3	15	30	60	90	120	150
3	0.7	7	35	70	140	210	280	350
4	1.2	12	60	120	240	360	480	600
5	1.9	19	95	190	380	570	760	950
6	2.7	27	135	270	540	810	1080	1350
7	3.6	36	180	360	720	1080	1440	1800
8	4.7	47	235	470	940	1410	1880	2350
9	5.9	59	295	590	1180	1770	2360	
10	7.2	72	360	720	1440	2160		
11	8.6	86	430	860	1720	2580		
12	10.2	102	510	1020	2040			
13	11.9	119	595	1190	2380			
14	13.7	137	685	1370	2740			
15	15.6	156	780	1560				
16	17.7	177	885	1770				
17	19.9	199	995	1990				
18	22.2	222	1110	2220				
19	24.6	246	1230	2460				
20	27.2	272	1360	2720				

Appendix 6 - Examples of Weight Units

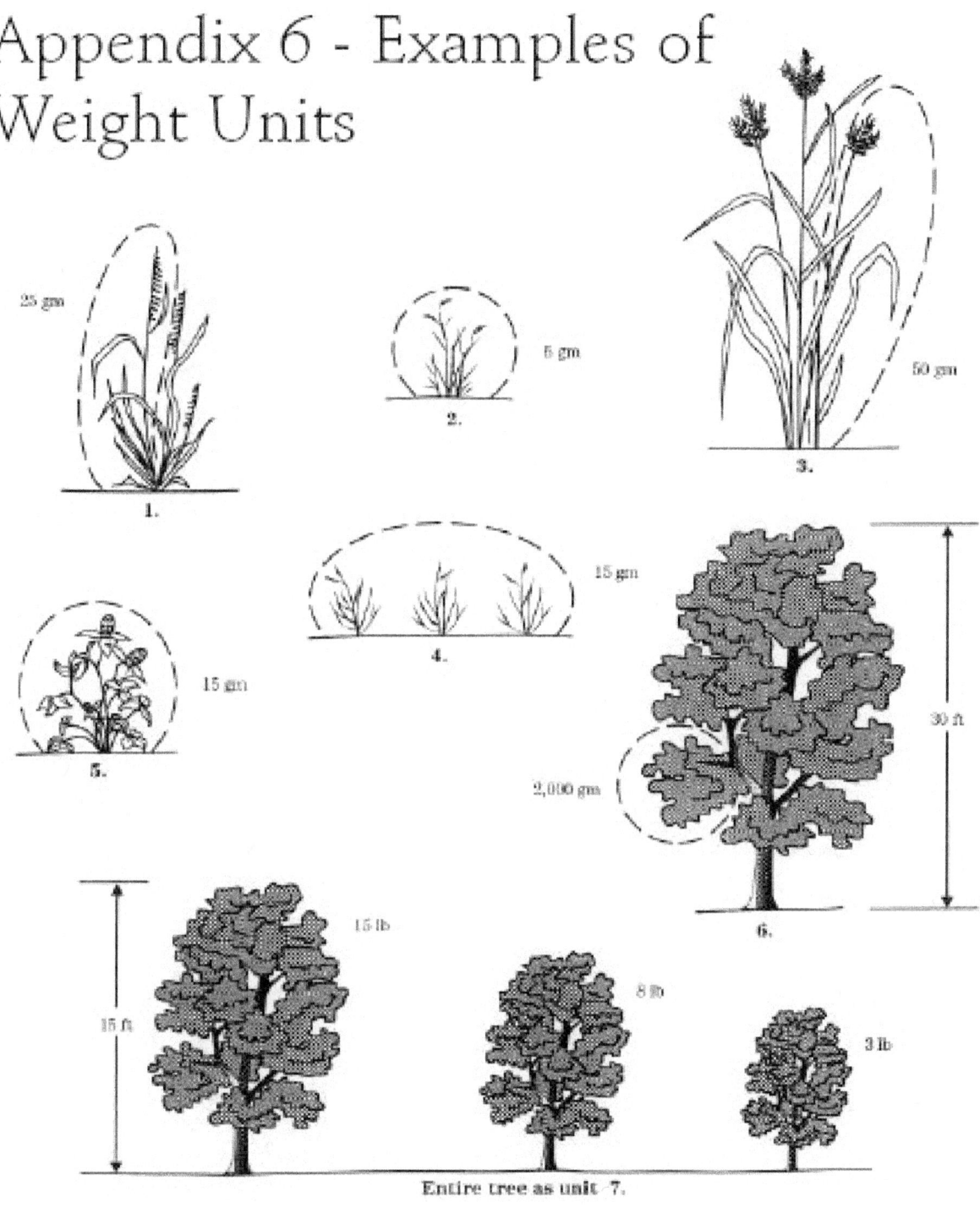

25 gm

5 gm

50 gm

15 gm

15 gm

2,000 gm

30 ft

15 lb

8 lb

3 lb

15 ft

Entire tree as unit 7.

(Reprinted from 190-vi, NRPH, September 1977)

Appendix 7 - Percentage Air-dry Weight Conversion Table

Percentage of Air-dry Weight in Harvested Plant Material at Various Stages of Growth

Grasses	Before heading initial growth to boot stage (%)	Headed out: boot stage to flowering (%)	Seed ripe: leaf tips drying (%)	Leaves dry stems partly dry (%)	Apparent dormancy (%)
Cool season wheatgrasses perennial bromes bluegrasses prairie junegrass	35	45	60	85	95
Warm season Tall grasses bluestems indiangrass switchgrass	30	45	60	85	95
Midgrasses side-oats grama tabosa galleta	40	55	65	90	95
Short grasses blue grama buffalograss short three-awns	45	60	80	90	95

Trees	New leaf and twig growth until leaves are full size (%)	Older and full size green leaves (%)	Green fruit (%)	Dry fruit (%)
Evergreen conifers ponderosa pine, slash pine-longleaf pine Utah juniper rocky mountain juniper spruce	45	55	35	85
Live oak	40	55	40	85
Deciduous blackjack oak post oak hickory	40	50	35	85

USDA, National Resources Conservation Service, National Range and Pasture Handbook

Percentage of air dry matter (continued)

Shrubs	New leaf and twig growth until leaves are full size (%)	Older and full-size green leaves (%)	Green fruit (%)	Green fruit (%)	
Evergreen big sagebrush bitterbrush ephedra algerita gallberry	55	65	35	85	
Deciduous snowberry rabbitbrush snakeweed Gambel oak mesquite	35	50	30	85	
Yucca and yucca like plants yucca sotol saw-palmetto	55	65	35	85	

Forbs	Initial growth to flowering (%)	Flowering to seed maturity (%)	Seed ripe leaf tips dry (%)	Leaves dry stems drying (%)	Dry (%)
Succulent violet waterleaf buttercup bluebells onion, lilies	15	35	60	90	100
Leafy Lupine lespedeza compassplant balsamroot tickclover	20	40	60	90	100
Fibrous leaves or mat phlox, mat eriogonum pussytoes	30	50	75	90	100

Succulents	New growth pads and fruit (%)	Older pads (%)	Old growth in dry years (%)
Prickly pear and barrel cactus	10	10	15+
Cholla cactus	20	25	30+

Appendix 8 - Vegetation Types and Subtypes

Information Resource Management (IRM) Codes for Vegetation Types and Subtypes

Type	Subtype	Code	Type	Subtype	Code
Annual Forbs		0000		Sand Sage	4046
	Filaree	0001		Chamise	4051
	Halogeton	0002		Manzanita	4052
	Other Forbs	0999		Ceanothus	4053
Grass		1000		Shinnery Oak	4054
	Short Grass	1001		Chaparral	4055
	Mid Grass	1002		Mountain Mahogany	4056
	Tall Grass	1003		Bitterbrush	4057
	Crested Wheat Grass	1004		Oakbrush	4058
	Mixed Grass Seeding	1005		Serviceberry	4059
	Other Grass	1999		Mountain shrub	4060
Grasslike	Sedge	2001		Blackbrush	4061
	Rush	2002		Cactus	4062
	Other Grasslike	2999		Joshua Tree	4063
Perennial Forbs		3001		Yucca	4064
Shrub		4000		White Thorn	4065
	Black Greasewood	4001		Paloverde Cerci	4066
	Bailey Greasewood	4002		Bursage FRDE-FRD	4067
	Creosote Bush	4011		Catclaw	4068
	Tarbush	4012		Sotol	4069
	Broom Dalea	4013		Mariola	4070
	Winterfat	4015		Snakeweed	4071
	Mesquite	4021		Fringed Sagebrush	4072
	Shadscale	4031		Clubmoss	4073
	Nuttal Saltbush	4032		Willow	4074
	Mat Saltbush	4033		Turpentine Brush	4075
	Fourwing Saltbush	4034		Burroweed HATE	4076
	Other Saltbush	4035		Mormon Tea	4077
	Desert Saltbush AT	4036		Skunk Bush	4078
	Mixed Desert Shrub	4037		Ocotilla	4079
	Big Sagebrush	4041		Sacahuiste	4080
	Low Sagebrush	4042		Alder	4081
	Black Sagebrush	4043		Snowberry	4082
	Other Sagebrush	4044		Other Shrub	4999
	Rabbitbrush	4045			

Information Resource Management (IRM) Codes for Vegetation Types and Subtypes (continued)

Type	Subtype	Code	Type	Subtype	Code
Broadleaf Trees		5000		Black Spruce	6043
	Willow	5074		Mountain Hemlock	6047
	Desert Willow	5075		Western Hemlock	6048
	Birch AK	5077		Alaskan Cedar	6049
	Balsam Pop - Cottoseed	5079		Western Larch	6055
	Red Alder	5081		Grand Fir- Larch-Doug Fir	6056
	Poplar - Birch	5082		Pond Pine- Larch-Doug Fir	6057
	Aspen	5083		Larch -Tamarack- Alaska	6058
	Calif Black Oak	5084		Lodgepole Pine	6061
	Cottonwood	5085		Redwood	6071
	Maple	5086		Noncommerical Softwood	6090
	Oregon White Oak	5087		Coulter Pine	6091
	Madrone	5088		Digger Pine	6092
	Tan Oak	5089		Pinyon-Juniper	6093
	Noncommercial Hardwood	5098		Knobcone Pine	6094
	Other Broadleaf Tree	5999		Bristlecone Pine	6095
Conifers		6000		Whitebk & Limber	6096
	Douglas Fir	6001		Pinyon	6097
	Doug Fir - Hemlock	6002		Juniper	6098
	Port Orford Cedar	6003		Commercial Nonstocked	6099
	Doug Fir - White Fir	6004		Other Conifer	6999
	Ponderosa Pine	6011	Cryptogams		7000
	Jeffery Pine	6012		Lichen-Moss	7001
	Pond-Sugar-Pine-Fir	6013		Moss	7002
	Sugar Pine	6014		Lichen	7003
	Incense Cedar	6015		Fern	7004
	Cypress	6019		Other	7999
	Western White Pine	6021	Barren		8000
	White Fir	6031	Annual grass		9000
	Red Fir	6032		Cheatgrass	9001
	Grand Fir	6033		Medusahead Rye	9002
	Pacific Silver Fir	6034		Red Brome	9003
	Engel Spruce	6035		Three-Awn	9005
	Engel Spruce- Subalp Fir	6036		Six Weeks grama	9006
	White Spruce	6037		Other	9999
	Blue Spruce	6038			
	Noble Fir	6039			
	Western Red Cedar	6041			
	Sitka Spruce	6042			

Appendix 9 - Similarity Index Form

Management Unit or Allotment _____ Examiner _____

Ecological Site _____ Location _____

Reference Plant Community _____ Date _____

A Plant Group	B Species Name	C Production/acres in reference plant community (from ecological site description)	D Annual production in lb/acre (actual or reconstructed)	E Pounds allowable
TOTALS				

SIMILARITY INDEX to Native Midgrass Community =
(Total of E divided by total of C)

Appendix 10 - Data Element Codes

A complete listing of all data elements can be found in the Corporate Data Dictionary at:
http://sc2962.sc.blm.gov/datashopper/default.asp

Data Element Landform 5132

Code	Landform Name	Description
ALF	ALLUVIAL FAN	The fan like deposit of a steam where it issues from a gorge upon a plain.
ARY	ARROYO	
BAL	BADLANDS	An area characterized by the intricate and sharp erosional sculpture of generally weak rocks forming nearly horizontal beds.
BNC	BENCH	Level narrow platform breaking up slope
BTT	BUTTE	An isolated hill or small mountain with steep sides. With a smaller summit area than a mesa.
CAN	CANYON	A deep narrow valley with precipitous sides where downward cutting of the stream greatly exceeds weathering.
CHL	CHANNEL	The bed of a single or braided watercourse that is commonly barren of vegetation.
CIN	CINDER CONE	
CRT	CREST	The very narrow commonly linear top of an erosional ridge, hill, mountain.
DMR	DRY MEADOW RIPARIAN	
FAN	FAN PIEDMONT	The most extensive major landform of most piedmont slopes, formed by the lateral coalescense of mountain-front alluvial fans downslope into one generally smooth slope without the transverse undulations of the semi-conical alluvial fans by accretion of fans aprons.
FPL	FLOOD PLAIN	A flat surface that may be submerged by waterflow built up by stream deposition.
GUL	GULLY	Gullies, arroyos, wadis, and gulches.
HBK	HOGBACK	A ridge of land formed by the outcropping edges of tilted strata; a ridge with a sharp summit and steeply sloping sides.
ISR	INTERMITTENT STREAM	

Code	Landform Name	Description
ITB	INTERMONTANE BASIN	A relatively small structural depression within a mountain range that is partly filled with alluvium and commonly drains externally through a narrower mountain valley.
MAN	LAVA FLOW- NONVEGETATED	
MAV	LAVA FLOW- VEGETATED	
MSA	MESA	An isolated hill or mountain having abrupt or steeply sloping sides and a level top.
MTN	MOUNTAIN	A steep elevation with a restricted summit area projecting 1000 feet or more above the surrounding land surface.
OLR	LAKE RIPARIAN	
ORR	RESERVOIR RIPARIAN	
OSR	STREAM RIPARIAN	
PED	PEDIMENT	A broad, gently sloping bedrock surface with low relief that is situated at the foot of a much steeper mountain slope.
PYA	PLAYA	An undrained basin that becomes at times a shallow lake on which evaporation may leave a deposit of salt.
RAV	RAVINE	Larger than a gully, smaller than a valley.
RDG	RIDGE	A range of hills or mountains or the upper part of such a range; an extended elevation between valleys.
SDL	SADDLE	A ridge connecting two higher elevations; a low point in the crestline of a ridge.
SDN	SAND DUNE	Sand dunes and sand hills.
SRP	SCARP	A line of cliffs produced by faulting or erosion.
SUM	SUMMIT	The flattish top of a an erosional fan remnant, hill, or mountain.
SWL	SWALE	
TRC	TERRACE	A level and ordinarily rather narrow plain usually with a steep front bordering a river, a lake, or the sea.
UPL	UPLANDS	High land especially far from the sea; ground elevated above the lowlands along rivers.
VAL	VALLEY	An elongated depression of the earth's surface commonly situated between ranges or hills or mountains and often comprising a drainage area and an area of generally flat land and drained or watered by a large river and its tributary streams.
WMR	WET MEADOW- RIPARIAN	

Soil Phase -
Texture Class 4991

Code	Texture Class
C	CLAY
CL	CLAY LOAM
COS	COARSE SAND
COSL	COARSE SANDY LOAM
FS	FINE SAND
FSL	FINE SANDY LOAM
L	LOAM
LCOS	LOAMY COARSE SAND
LFS	LOAMY FINE SAND
LS	LOAMY SAND
LVSF	LOAMY VERY FINE SAND
S	SAND
SC	SANDY CLAY
SCL	SANDY CLAY LOAM
SI	SILT
SIC	SILTY CLAY
SICL	SILTY CLAY LOAM
SIL	SILT LOAM
SL	SANDY LOAM
VFS	VERY FINE SAND
VFSL	VERY FINE SANDY LOAM

Soil Phase -
Texture Modifier data element 4992

Code	Texture Modifier
BY	Bouldery
BYV	Very Bouldery
BYX	Extremely Bouldery
CB	Cobbly
CBA	Angular Cobbly
CBV	Very Cobbly
CBX	Extremely Cobbly
CN	Chennery
CNV	Very Chennery
CNX	Extremely Chennery
CR	Cherty
CRC	Coarse Cherty
CRV	Very Cherty
CRX	Extremely Cherty
FL	Flaggy
FLV	Very Flaggy
FLX	Extremely Flaggy
GR	Gravelly
GRC	Coarse Gravelly
GRF	Fine Gravelly
GRV	Very Gravelly
GRX	Extremely Gravelly
MK	Mucky
PT	peaty
RB	Rubbly
SH	Shaly
SHV	Very Shaly
SHX	Extremely Shaly
SR	Stratified
ST	Stony
STV	Very Stony
STX	Extremely Stony
SY	Slaty
SYV	Very Slaty
SYX	Extremely Slaty

REPORT DOCUMENTATION PAGE

Form Approved
OMB No. 0704-0188

Public reporting burden for this collection of information is estimated to average 1 hour per response, including the time for reviewing instructions, searching existing data sources, gathering and maintaining the data needed, and completing and reviewing the collection of information. Send comments regarding this burden estimate or any other aspect of this collection of information, including suggestions for reducing this burden, to Washington Headquarters Services, Directorate for Information Operations and Reports, 1215 Jefferson Davis Highway, Suite 1204, Arlington, VA 22202-4302, and to the Office of Management and Budget, Paperwork Reduction Project (0704-0188), Washington, DC 20503.

1. AGENCY USE ONLY (leave blank)	2. REPORT DATE Dec. 2001	3. REPORT TYPE AND DATES COVERED Final

4. TITLE AND SUBTITLE

Inventory and Monitoring—Technical Reference 1734-7
Ecological Site Inventory

5. FUNDING NUMBERS

6. AUTHOR(S)

Edward F. Habich

7. PERFORMING ORGANIZATION NAME(S) AND ADDRESS(ES)

U.S. Department of the Interior
Bureau of Land Management
National Science and Technology Center
P.O. Box 25047
Denver, CO 80225-0047

8. PERFORMING ORGANIZATION REPORT NUMBER

BLM/ST/ST-01/003+1734

9. SPONSORING/MONITORING AGENCY NAME(S) AND ADDRESS(ES)

10. SPONSORING/MONITORING AGENCY REPORT NUMBER

11. SUPPLEMENTARY NOTES

12a. DISTRIBUTION/AVAILABILITY STATEMENT

12b. DISTRIBUTION CODE

13. ABSTRACT (Maximum 200 words)

Technical Reference 1734-7 describes the procedures for planning and conducting ecological site inventories and for documenting ecological site descriptions. It includes detailed information about mapping ecological sites and plant communities. It includes information about the collection of vegetation production data and the use of the data for determining a similarity index. It discusses plant succession and state and transition pathways.

14. SUBJECT TERMS

vegetation production, soil map units, vegetation mapping, ecological sites, state and transition pathways, site write-up area, stratification, vegetation subtypes, similarity index

15. NUMBER OF PAGES

128 including covers

16. PRICE CODE

17. SECURITY CLASSIFICATION OF REPORT Unclassified	18. SECURITY CLASSIFICATION OF THIS PAGE Unclassified	19. SECURITY CLASSIFICATION OF ABSTRACT Unclassified	20. LIMITATION OF ABSTRACT UL

NSN 7540-01-280-5500

Standard Form 298 (Rev. 2-89)
Prescribed by ANSI Std. Z39-18
298-102